D0753554

BUILDING AMERICA
THEN AND NOW

THE
ALASKA HIGHWAY

BUILDING AMERICA: THEN AND NOW

BUILDING AMERICA
THEN AND NOW

THE

ALASKA HIGHWAY

PAUL KUPPERBERG

CHELSEA HOUSE
PUBLISHERS
An imprint of Infobase Publishing

The Alaska Highway

Copyright © 2009 by Infobase Publishing

All rights reserved. No part of this book may be reproduced or utilized in any form or by any means, electronic or mechanical, including photocopying, recording, or by any information storage or retrieval systems, without permission in writing from the publisher. For information contact:

Chelsea House
An imprint of Infobase Publishing
132 West 31st Street
New York, NY 10001

Library of Congress Cataloging-in-Publication Data
Kupperberg, Paul.
    The Alaska Highway / by Paul Kupperberg.
        p. cm. — (Building America : then and now)
    Includes bibliographical references and index.
    ISBN 978-1-60413-074-4 (hardcover : alk. paper)
    1. Alaska Highway—History—Juvenile literature. 2. Roads—Alaska—Design and construction—History—Juvenile literature. 3. Roads—British Columbia—Design and construction—History—Juvenile literature. 4. Roads—Yukon—Design and construction—History—Juvenile literature. 5. United States. Army. Corps of Engineers—History—Juvenile literature. I. Title. II. Series.
    F1060.92.K87 2009
    388.109798—dc22   2008025547

Chelsea House books are available at special discounts when purchased in bulk quantities for businesses, associations, institutions, or sales promotions. Please call our Special Sales Department in New York at (212) 967-8800 or (800) 322-8755.

You can find Chelsea House on the World Wide Web at http://www.chelseahouse.com

Text design by Annie O'Donnell
Cover design by Ben Peterson

Printed in the United States of America

Bang NMSG 10 9 8 7 6 5 4 3 2 1

This book is printed on acid-free paper.

All links and Web addresses were checked and verified to be correct at the time of publication. Because of the dynamic nature of the Web, some addresses and links may have changed since publication and may no longer be valid.

CONTENTS

"Imperative from the Viewpoint of National Defense"

O n December 7, 1941, the American naval base at Pearl Harbor, Hawaii, was attacked by the Japanese air force, devastating the nation's Pacific Fleet and drawing the United States into the global conflict that became World War II.

The attack on the future fiftieth state of the Union had an impact that was felt around the world, including in the farthest reaches of the future forty-ninth state, Alaska. A little more than three months after the bombs fell on those American ships, the first of more than 18,000 U.S. military personnel and civilian workers and countless tons of equipment were hastily mobilized and shipped across Canada and Alaska in a massive effort to prevent future attacks on America or its interests by the Japanese.

Hawaii and Alaska could not have been more diverse. Tropical Hawaii is located in the middle of the North Pacific Ocean, whereas Alaska is half the world away in the Arctic tundra. The one thing they had in common with each other, and with Japan, was the Pacific Ocean.

Japan had Pacific military bases only 750 miles (1,207 kilometers) from the southwestern tip of Alaska's Aleutian Islands, a chain of more than 300 volcanic islands that extends west from the southern tip of Alaska. America was vulnerable to attack by Japan from the north: A Japanese military force would need only to make the short trip to the Aleutians and, from there, cross the Bering Sea and head south through Alaska and Canada to attack the North American West Coast.

America recognized the sorry state of its defenses in Alaska. The Soviet Union was reportedly building air bases on islands in the Bering Strait only one and a half miles from Alaska. General Billy Mitchell, the controversial advocate of increased American air power and developer of the aircraft carrier who predicted the Japanese attack on Pearl Harbor in 1924, also saw Alaska as a weak link in America's Pacific defenses.

The United States, which had purchased the 663,267 square miles (1,717,854 sq km) of Alaska from Russia in 1867 for $7.2 million, had only a marginal military presence in the territory through the 1930s. In 1940, the population of Alaska was 72,000; only a handful of air, naval, and communications bases and outposts had been set up, including a small naval base at Dutch Harbor in the Aleutians.

As a result of the worsening situation in Europe, both the United States and Canada began to make plans for the defense of North America. When France fell to the Germans in June 1940, the neighboring nations set up the Canadian-American Permanent Joint Board of Defense (PJBD) to manage all North American defense policies. Among the board's first actions was to approve the Northwest Staging Route, a series of airports, airstrips, and radio directional stations every 100 miles (160 km) stretching from British Columbia, across the Yukon, and into Alaska. It also approved the Alaska Highway, designed to provide a direct land route to Alaska that linked together the chain of Staging Route airfields and bases.

The Northwest Staging Route was deemed essential to North America's Pacific defense strategy as well as to the war in Europe and the rest of the world. The route and the Alaska Highway were used to ferry equipment and supplies to Russia to fight the attacking Germans as part of the Lend-Lease Program, a system devised by President Franklin Delano Roosevelt that allowed isolationist America to "lend" the embattled Russians (as well as other allies, including Great Britain) equipment without actually taking sides and entering the war against the German, Japanese, and Italian axis.

The route was also of primary importance in the event of a Japanese attack from the north. Without a system of air bases and communications lines and an open, continuous route along which to move men and supplies, the advantage was in the hands of the hypothetical invaders.

In anticipation of the coming conflict, the Canadian government began work on the Staging Route in early 1941. In order to create a new airfield several miles west of Fort Nelson, the first link in the route, men and equipment were sent 300 miles (483 km) to Dawson Creek, British Columbia, by rail on the Northern Alberta Railway. From there, they traveled 50 miles (80 km) through the wilderness and across the frozen Peace River to Fort St. John. Bulldozers widened and improved the sparse winter trails to Fort Nelson so that the necessary heavy equipment and trucks could begin their work on this vital airstrip.

The United States began construction of two airfields in Alaska—one at Big Delta, located 100 miles (160 km) outside of Fairbanks, and the other at Northway, near the border with Canada. These bases, closer to centers of population, presented far fewer challenges in their construction. Yet, as the year wore on and tensions between America and Japan worsened, the Northwest Staging Route became—in the words of a PJBD recommendation—"of extreme importance."

Ironically, a 1941 article in the Japanese newspaper *Hochi* reported that the Japanese government had declared the "string of air bases . . . built along the highway . . . will be regarded as a continuation of the horseshoe-shaped encirclement of Japan by the Washington government. Military bases of the United States

The Alaska Highway was built to strengthen the infrastructure of Alaska and prevent attacks from invading nations. The U.S. military assigned soldiers to the task of constructing the highway. *Above,* the SS *David W. Branch* carries troops into the Gulf of Alaska.

would thus be strategic from Singapore via Australia, the Philippines, Hawaii and the United States to Canada and Alaska." Before the year was out, the Japanese government in Tokyo would further express its displeasure via its actions at Pearl Harbor.

By 1941, about 20,000 American troops were stationed in Alaska, although they were not sufficiently prepared. Alaska was home to fewer than three dozen bombers and fighters, only half of which were operational. General Simon Buckner, the commander of the Alaska Defense Command, reported to Washington, D.C., that he did not have the resources to defend the territory in the event of an invasion. As late as September 1941, he informed Washington, "Due to the utter lack of roads and railroad . . . the Army garrison cannot be regarded as anything but local defense forces. There is no existing means now of determining when or where the enemy is coming and no means of stopping his approach if we know it."

Despite dire warnings, General Buckner's requests for additional men and equipment to protect naval bases and airfields—particularly the Dutch Harbor facilities in the vulnerable Aleutians—were turned down. The War Department (as the U.S. Department of Defense was then called) was not willing to commit its resources to these distant locales before the Japanese committed any openly hostile acts.

According to an official of the War Department in the February 7, 1942, edition of the *New York Times*, "The military and naval situation in the Pacific now indicates that a land route alternative to the existing sea routes is desirable from the viewpoint of national defense." The article went on to say that, although such a road "has been a subject of Cabinet discussions . . . there is a belief within the Cabinet, said to be shared by President Roosevelt, that the project could be carried through by the Chief Executive even without Congressional approval of legislation if the Government of Canada approved."

With defense foremost on everyone's mind, President Roosevelt needed no convincing when the plan for the highway to Alaska landed on his desk. On February 11, 1942, he authorized the project to begin immediately. It was, according to Secretary of War Henry Stimson, "imperative from the viewpoint of national defense."

Due to the severity of the northern weather, it was equally imperative that work begin immediately, to take advantage of the spring and summer seasons. Once winter set in, with its blizzards and –30°F (–34°C) temperatures that made it dangerous for men to work outside and left machines unable to operate, work would grind to a halt. Neither the American nor the Canadian government wished to leave this vital project on hold for any reason. The highway would stretch across more than 1,600 miles (2,575 km) of some of Canada's and Alaska's most rugged, uncharted terrain—over mountains, through valleys, and around or across gorges and great bodies of water. In addition, the project had to be completed in just eight months, which meant that *seven miles* of road had to be built every day.

It was an impossible task that would take an army of men and equipment to achieve. Yet, with the world at war and America's security at stake, the impossible would just have to become routine.

CHAPTER 1

"It Was Nothing but Indian Trails"

The idea of a highway that connected the United States and Canada with the far northern territories did not spring full-blown from the minds of the War Department following Pearl Harbor. At the turn of the nineteenth century, influential American railroad tycoon F.H. Harriman dreamed of a rail line that would run through Canada and Alaska to link up with the Russian railroad by tunneling under, or bridging, the Bering Strait. The 1904 defeat of Russia in the Russo-Japanese War put an end to Harriman's dream. The following year, however, a North West Mounted Police officer named Major Constantine was sent to open a trail to the gold fields of the Canadian Yukon; he managed to build 375 miles (603 km) of road between Fort St. John and the Stikine River before the project was cancelled.

PROMOTING THE ALASKAN HIGHWAY

Donald MacDonald, the location engineer of the Alaska Road Commission headquartered in Fairbanks, Alaska, also dreamed of a highway to Alaska and made his proposal for one in 1928.

MacDonald's original plan was ambitious; the road would have ultimately run from Alaska to equatorial Panama and the canal there, linking the Pacific and Atlantic oceans. The military advantage of such a route was obvious. The United States, however—in the throes of the unprecedented prosperity and, more importantly, peace following the first World War—did not see any immediate need for a highway from the southern tip of one continent to the northern edge of another.

The world had changed by 1933, when Congress authorized President Roosevelt to initiate a joint U.S.-Canadian commission to study a road to Alaska. The commission existed in part as a response to the International Highway Association, a group headed by Donald MacDonald. MacDonald was not above promoting the highway scheme with stunts. He encouraged an Alaskan fur trapper, Clyde "Slim" Williams, to make good on a boast that he could make the trip from Alaska to Seattle, a route largely without roads, by motorcycle.

According to an article in the February 2000 issue of the Alaskan Bureau of Land Management's publication, *Frontiers*, Williams and his partner, John Logan, took off on May 14, 1939, from Fairbanks, Alaska: "The pair had 'help from all sides,' (according to Williams) including Donald MacDonald's son, Donald III, who helped by assembling maps and attaching them to canvas for durability. The pair was presented with a young Siberian Husky named Blizzard." Five months later, Williams, Logan, and Blizzard rode onto the existing U.S. highway system and were hailed as heroes. Williams continued on to the 1939 World's Fair in Chicago, where he and Blizzard were a popular attraction, and then to Washington, D.C., to meet President Roosevelt.

A highway to Alaska was suddenly a popular topic. It offered many benefits, including, according to MacDonald in a January 12, 1939, *New York Times* article, "an opportunity for every American motorist to visit the territory where tennis is played in mid-summer until 11 P.M., where trout thirty-six inches long are a nuisance, and where a hunter, miner or farmer pays no tax on the land he owns." The same article pointed out how long MacDonald had been beating the drum for this project: "Since 1927 such a highway has been Mr. MacDonald's aim . . . but financial difficulties have stood in the way. 'We need $12,000,000 to $15,000,000, but what's that today?' [MacDonald] asked."

The joint U.S.-Canadian Alaskan International Highway Commission reported on November 7, 1939, that the highway was, in fact, a " 'worthy and feasible project' of reasonable cost," according to the *Times*. The commission recommended Blaine, Washington, as "the most feasible contact point between the United States and Canada."

MacDonald also made sure that the American public understood that his highway was more than just a tourist attraction. As reported in the *New York Times* on August 26, 1940, he brought home the idea of Alaska's vulnerability. "Three men with a fishing boat . . . could paralyze the United States defense machine in less than an hour, in the opinion of Donald MacDonald, Alaska Highway Commission engineer," the article warned. MacDonald was quoted as pointing to the territory's only all-weather port, Seward, as most vulnerable. Saboteurs could cripple the port with "a series of explosions. One would be the oil tanks near the only wharf. Alaska's entire gas and oil supply is there, with no reserve anywhere. The next would be the wharf itself."

American concerns about an attack were justified when, only months later, on June 3, 1942, the Japanese attacked the American base at Dutch Harbor in the Aleutians. More than 100 Americans were killed in the battle, which lasted less than a week. When it was over, the Japanese held two islands at the western end of the island chain—the first time since the War of 1812 that enemy forces had captured American territory. Both the military and residents of Alaska believed that the enemy's next step would be an invasion of North America through Alaska via the stepping-stone of the Aleutian Islands.

Long before then, however, the United States International Highway Commission and its Canadian counterpart had been convened. German and Japanese military aggression was by

After the Japanese attack on Pearl Harbor, President Roosevelt (*above,* signing a declaration of war against Germany) realized shipping routes around Alaska and Canada also were vulnerable. The president made the Alaska Highway project a top priority, in order to create an alternative method of transporting supplies to military bases.

then a serious enough threat that the defense of Alaska became a priority.

American shipping—vital to the war effort—was threatened, not just out at sea but close to home as well. During the first two months of the war, dozens of visual and radio sightings of Japanese naval activity were reported off the American West Coast and in the Gulf of Alaska. Sixteen Japanese submarine attacks caused damage to six freighters and tankers, and two American ships were sunk. America's Pacific naval fleet had been decimated by the attack on Pearl Harbor, and it would be a long time before it was rebuilt and could provide protection to supply ships. The navy had only five destroyers available to serve as escorts to convoys of ships and to scout for the Japanese submarines that threatened them.

Shipping would be the primary method of transporting the necessary supplies to the north and, from there, to Europe, but an air route was deemed just as important. The Northwest Staging Route was still new, and it relied on a few scattered and under-equipped airfields with inadequate radio and navigational facilities. These conditions were highlighted in January 1942, when the first group of U.S. warplanes was sent over the Northwest Staging Route. Of the 38 planes in the flight, 27 crashed along the way. The severe northern weather and the inexperienced pilots were partly to blame for the disaster, but much of the problem was attributed to the long distances between airfields and a lack of adequate navigational aids over strange and hostile territory. The need for an overland route to service the Staging Route had never been greater or more immediate.

The president's commission met to appoint a slate of commissioners that included Alaska's Donald MacDonald; Washington State congressman Warren Magnuson; Oregon's public works administrator F.W. Carey; Alaska's ex-governor Thomas Riggs; and Canadians Thomas Tremblay, Charles Stewart, and J.M. Wardle. The first order of business was to plan the route of this ambitious project.

EAST OR WEST?

The joint American-Canadian commission had, in fact, very few options in their choice of a route. The main objective was to cut a road through Canada and Alaska to link a string of military installations that stretched from Edmonton, Alberta, to Fairbanks, Alaska. It would form a supply chain to Europe and Asia and a defensive wall against invasion. The route was, for the most part, dictated by the location of the bases and installations it would service.

Initially, there was discussion of constructing a rail line, which offered a greater capacity for cargo than did a road. Laying tracks through the wilderness, however, was deemed too time-consuming and expensive. As it was initially envisioned, the two-lane gravel road that could connect the existing U.S. highway system to distant Fairbanks, Alaska, would be difficult enough to build on its own. Early estimates had the project taking two years to complete at a cost of between $50,000 and $60,000 per mile.

At the outset, four proposed routes were under consideration. Some were longer than others but offered disadvantages in such matters as terrain, weather, or location. The road had several separate but distinct needs, including having to pass as close as possible to many points on the map where existing airfields and other facilities were already located; relative ease of travel through harsh terrain, Arctic weather conditions, and mountains; access to connecting sea and rail facilities so that men and machines could be brought in; and being located far enough inland that it was not vulnerable to attack from the sea.

Not one of the four routes, known as Routes A, B, C, and D, offered everything that was needed. In fact, *none* answered the greatest need of running parallel to the string of seven Northwest Staging Route airfields the road was being built to link.

The United States favored Route A, which started in British Columbia at Prince George, and then cut northwest to Hazelton and up the Stikine River to White Horse and Fairbanks by way of the Tanana Valley. Although this was advantageous because it provided a direct connection between Seattle, Washington, and Alaska, it ran parallel to the West Coast for 150 miles (240 km), which made it vulnerable to attack from the sea. It also bypassed several air bases and went through areas of high snowfall at steep grades, or angles of elevation.

The Canadians favored Route B, a longer, more expensive route that covered more ground in Canadian territory. Route B also started in Prince George, but then it traveled through the Rocky Mountain Trench before extending to Dawson City and then down the Yukon Valley to Fairbanks. From the American point of view, this route, which did not connect the air bases it was intended to link and could take up to six years to complete, was not a viable option.

So, military planners added a fifth option to the list—a hybrid of Routes A and C, with a new stretch of road thrown in for good measure. The points along the Northwest Staging Route could be serviced by following 630 miles (1,014 km) of the southern part of Route C to Watson Lake and then crossing the Rocky Mountains and continuing on to Whitehorse. There it would link up with Route A, another 300 miles (483 km) of distance, for the final 500 miles (805 km) to an existing stretch of road known as the Richardson Highway, which began at Big Delta.

When Colonel (later General) William M. Hoge arrived in Alaska on Valentine's Day of 1942 to inspect the proposed route and take command of the Alaska-Canada highway project, the decision of *where* to cross the mountains had still not been made. "We didn't know where we were going actually at that time, but I knew we had to go to Fort Nelson (a small town in the northeast corner of British Columbia)," General Hoge, who died in 1979, later recalled in memoirs published by the 1993 U.S. Army Corps of Engineers, *Engineer Memoirs: General William M. Hoge*. "We had only a few points in there we had to go."

Because of those "few points," the string of military bases and airfields the highway had to link, an easier route had to be bypassed. According to General Hoge,

If you wanted a better route, I think I would come up from Vancouver and go up the Rocky Mountain trench, which is due north and is a very peculiar trench in there that doesn't go very high. I think probably the highest elevation is 1,000 feet (660 meters) and that would have gone straight up to wherever we were headed for, which was Whitehorse. But we had to go to the airfields that were selected.

Though it met many of the military's criteria, the new route was far from perfect. Between Watson Lake and Whitehorse lay the Rocky Mountains. The Rockies, formed millions of years ago, stretch more than 3,000 miles (4,800 km) from New Mexico in the American Southwest to northern British Columbia in Canada. They reach as high as 14,400 feet (4,401 meters) at Colorado's Mount Elbert and 12,972 feet (3,954 km) at Mount Robson in British Columbia.

This great hump across the back of the North American continental Midwest was a formidable obstacle to an eastern or western route through—or, more accurately, *over*—the mountains. In truth, no one could say with any certainty that there even *was* a viable path through the mountains in the area the road had to travel. Even as construction began, the planners hoped they would have a solution to that problem by the time they had to face it.

MAPPING THE ROUTE

The Rockies were not the only area of uncertainty for the highway builders. Some portions of the route, such as the stretch between Whitehorse and Big Delta, were relatively well mapped. Southeast of Whitehorse, information was sparser and required aerial photography and teams of surveyors on the ground to fill in the many blank spots on the map. For the most part, the conditions of the land—including soil conditions, elevations, and gradients—were unknown. The builders would have to start rolling before their superiors knew exactly where they were

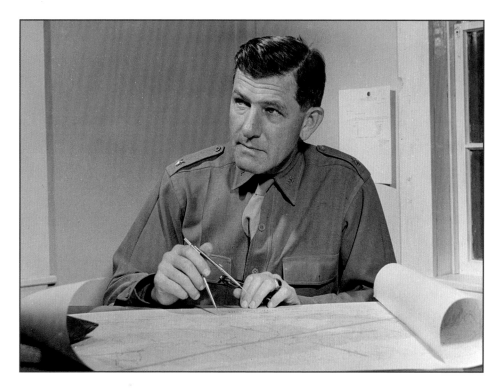

A respected engineer and military man, Colonel William M. Hoge *(above)* was given an almost impossible assignment when he was put in charge of the Alaska Highway project. Responsible for managing the work of seven regiments over a large area that was still mostly unmapped, Hoge arrived in Alaska and immediately went to work at establishing a planned route for the roadway.

going and what conditions they would encounter once they got there.

Surveyors began their scouting and mapping efforts as soon as a decision on the route was reached. The surveyors of Company D of the 29th Engineer Topographical Battalion and Company A of the 648th Engineers were the first ones in. Working with only a single map of the area between Dawson Creek and Fort Nelson and in conditions that included several feet of snow on the ground and dense clouds of mosquitoes and gnats, they pushed through the wilderness.

Even without the snow and insects, their job was not easy. While the first priority was to link the string of Alaskan and Yukon Territory airfields that the road was being built to service, they had the added difficulty of doing so in a way that avoided hazardous and impassable areas and steep terrain.

Reliable maps of the area did not exist at the time. "The airplane maps were about the best we had," said General Hoge. "I think a lot of them came out of *National Geographic Magazine*—they were scaled about 50 miles to the inch . . . so

GENERAL WILLIAM M. HOGE

William Hoge was born in Booneville, Missouri, on January 13, 1894, the middle of three sons in a military family. His father was headmaster of a small military school, and all three sons graduated from the U.S. Military Academy at West Point. William graduated twenty-ninth in a class of 125 and left his mark as a member of the academy's football team.

Hoge's grades earned him a commission in the prestigious Corps of Engineers, and he served in World War I as a highly decorated combat veteran. He earned the Distinguished Service Cross, the army's second highest award for valor, for his bravery under fire during a river-crossing operation. After the war, he earned a degree in civil engineering at the Massachusetts Institute of Technology and was then sent to the Command and General Staff School at Fort Leavenworth, Kansas, a sure step up the ladder of promotion.

From 1935 to 1937, Hoge commanded the 14th Engineer Battalion of the Philippine Scouts, where he gained road-building experience (that would later serve him in Alaska) by building a network of roads and bridges in the jungles of the Bataan Peninsula. From there, he worked on flood control measures in the Missouri River District and then went to the Engineer Training Center at Fort Belvoir, Virginia.

After nine months directing the construction of the Alaska Highway, during which he was promoted to the rank of brigadier general, William you know what was on them. All I knew was my points. I started at the end of the railroad . . . (at) Dawson Creek. From there I had to make a road into Fort Nelson." With little information to guide them, the best the chief of engineers could do was send Hoge and his men north with orders that they find a way to build a road that went from point A to point B. *How* they were to accomplish that and by which route was up to Hoge to determine.

The surveying teams consisted of one officer and nine survey-ors. The teams would break up into smaller groups, which would

Hoge was assigned to the Armored Force at Fort Knox, Kentucky. From there, he became commander of the 5th Engineer Special Brigade, which was to participate in the June 1944 Allied invasion of the European continent. General Hoge's command was instrumental in helping to secure the beach on D-Day, and he later participated in the Battle of the Bulge with the 9th Armored Division, an action that won him the Distinguished Service Medal. He was further decorated in 1945 and received a promotion to major general.

After World War II, General Hoge continued his service and earned further distinction and decorations, first as an engineer and then as the commanding general of U.S. troops in Trieste, Italy, and as commander of IX Corps during the Korean War following his promotion to lieutenant general. Before he retired in January 1955, General Hoge commanded the Fourth Army at Fort Sam Houston, Texas, and the Seventh Army in Germany. In September 1953, he received his fourth star as commander in chief of the U.S. Army in Europe.

General Hoge became chairman of the board of Interlake Iron Corporation of Cleveland, Ohio, and retired in 1965. In 1975, Hoge's health began to fail; he moved to Easton, Kansas, to live with his son, retired army colonel George F. Hoge. He died on October 29, 1979, at the age of 85, at Munson Army Hospital in Fort Leavenworth, Kansas.

travel a mile or so through the wilderness on different tracks to determine which route offered the best or easiest access. They would then backtrack and regroup to choose among the potential routes, which they would then mark for the following survey team. This second team would lay out the centerline and elevations of the route. On average, teams would make anywhere from two to four miles of progress a day, often with the help of the local Indian population as their guides. The advance parties were kept supplied by provisions brought in by dogsleds or horses.

When construction began, the surveying teams were still hard at work—often only miles ahead of the trailing road crews. As the bulldozers cut their way through the wilderness just behind them, the surveyors "would be exploring two or three possible valleys as to where the road would go, knowing that they had to find a route that could be built, because the bulldozers were right behind them and they were not about to stop," according to historian Heath Twichell—whose father served as an engineer on the highway project—in the "Building the Alaska Highway" episode of the PBS documentary series *American Experience*.

"This was a job for Paul Bunyan; to wrest an all-weather road from the jealous Northland between early spring and autumn," *Time* magazine reported in its August 31, 1942, issue. "To span the fierce, death-cold rushing rivers, the black custard quagmires; to cut switchbacks across the Great Divide, to make the way between the Arctic and the U.S. for a highway which someday may be as common as the Boston Post Road." The magazine told readers the challenge facing the U.S. Army Corps of Engineers was "one of the biggest and toughest jobs . . . since they built the Panama Canal. Almost no outsiders had penetrated the vast, still, endless wilderness where the engineers are wrenching and hacking a great military road 1,500 miles (2,414 km) from Fort St. John, B.C. to mid-Alaska."

Hoge inspected the army's proposed route in February 1942 when, according to *Time* magazine, "the land was deep in snow."

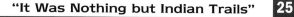

Alongside a construction expert for the Public Roads Administration (PRA) and a fellow officer, "they slogged through snow drifts, checking grades, rivers, elevations."

THE FIRST MILES

"It would take a long time to build from end to end," General Hoge recalled. "So, we had to find some ways of breaking (the highway) into segments."

While winter temperatures remained below freezing, the movement of men and heavy equipment was a chilling but relatively easy affair. They traveled along a 50-mile (80 km) dirt road and across the frozen 1,500-foot (457 m) Peace River. Once spring brought warmer weather, however, those 50 miles of dirt would be transformed into 50 miles of nearly impassable mud and the Peace River would become a raging torrent across which no bridge yet existed. Once that happened, the only route to Fort Nelson involved a 1,000-mile (1,609 km) trip by barge down the Mackenzie River.

By the time Hoge reported back to his superiors in Washington, D.C., that his assigned task was, in fact, possible, the army had less than six weeks to pack up the men and equipment of the 35th Engineer Regiment (Combat) waiting at Fort Ord, California, and deliver them to Dawson Creek via the Northern Alberta Railroad from Edmonton. They arrived on March 2, 1942, to get the work started.

The 340th General Service Regiment was sent ahead to build the road south, while the 341st General Service Regiment deployed to Fort St. John, where they would build the road to Fort Nelson and connect with the stretch of road to Fairbanks. The 18th Combat Regiment was sent to Whitehorse, where the men began the northwest leg of the highway toward Alaska and Fairbanks, the highway's northern terminus. Each regiment comprised about 2,000 men.

The 35th Engineers, which consisted primarily of men who had been drafted in anticipation of the coming war, faced its first test as a unit on the Alaska Highway. The men had performed admirably in earlier training maneuvers, but not until they hit Fort Nelson in Canada's British Columbia were they truly put to the test. The men were divided into teams that specialized in a particular job, such as the "F" Company, who were experts in preparing and loading the heavy equipment onto railcars. The military hierarchy was so impressed by the 35th Engineers that

BUILDING AMERICA NOW

STUART HIGHWAY: A HIGHWAY DOWN UNDER

Australia's Stuart Highway runs from the city of Darwin, the capitol of the country's Northern Territory, through the center of the continent to Port Augusta in southern Australia. Known as "the Track" since the route was first blazed in 1862, it took the threat of World War II to transform this rough path through the Australian wilderness into something more than a dirt road. Unlike the Alaska Highway, the 1,689-mile (2,719 km) route of the Stuart Highway had been determined more than a century before its construction, by nineteenth-century explorer John McDouall Stuart and British telegraph specialist Charles Todd, who emigrated to South Australia in November 1855.

Australia is a 2,941,299-square-mile (7,617,930 square km) landmass in the Southern Hemisphere surrounded by the Pacific and Indian oceans. Inhabited by indigenous people for an estimated 42,000 to 48,000 years, Australia was first sighted by the Europeans in 1606, by a Dutch navigator named Willem Janszoon. British explorer James Cook mapped the east coast of the country, which he named New South Wales, in 1770. The British began to settle the country in 1778, first as a penal colony for deported criminals and later by free settlers they presented them as the model for other engineering units to emulate and chose them as among the first to be assigned the vital task of building the Alaska Highway.

"There were never enough trucks to move (supplies)," *Time* magazine reported. "Farmers, garagemen, merchants, traders piled in with their own vehicles. All the short days and long nights the trucks mired down in slush, were dug out, pushed on."

whose protests against the use of their land as a prison led to an end to that practice in 1848.

Over time, and as the population increased during the nineteenth century, colonies were settled in other territories across Australia, including Victoria, Queensland, South Australia, the Northern Territory, and Queensland. These six self-governing territories joined to form a federation in 1901, creating the Commonwealth of Australia. It remained a dominion of the British Empire until 1942, however, when the country ended most of its formal constitutional links with England.

During most of its history, the majority of Australia's European citizens remained confined to the coastal areas of the continent. The vast interior of Australia comprises desert or semi-arid lands, and temperate climates exist only in its southeastern and southwestern corners. Australia is mostly flat and is the driest of the world's inhabited continents. So remote and inhospitable are these interior lands, known as the Outback, that more than 70 years after it was first settled Europeans still had no idea what lay at the heart of their new land. One common belief was that a great inland sea stood at the center of the continent, but attempts to explore this harsh land were met with failure and, often, death. Not until 1862 was a successful south-to-north crossing of Australia achieved; this paved the way not only for the opening of the Northern Territory and the mysteries of the interior, but also for a highway across the continent.

By April, however, "the effort seemed not enough. A sudden thaw set the river ice groaning and cracking like pistol shots. Trucks crossed only in the middle hours of the night. Came a late hard freeze and the last truck was over." The first hurdle to this massive undertaking had been passed.

Yet, it was far from the last hurdle this project would face. The logistics of building the great road were staggering, and the Canadian government left the task in the hands of Colonel Hoge and his men. As its contribution, Canada provided the United States with the right of way through its territory; a permit to take timber, gravel, and rock from public lands; and a waiver of import duties, sales and income taxes, and immigration laws for laborers, as well as approximately $80 million of manpower and equipment.

The first miles were rough ones. When we think of a highway today, we envision modern six- or eight-lane roads paved in asphalt or concrete that are well-drained, lighted, and pitched at a gradual grade to allow for ease of driving by civilian traffic.

By *that* definition, the first stretches of the Alaska Highway were no more than glorified pioneer trails. They were rough, muddy swatches cut through woods by bulldozer and hand. They were built across muddy plains and over steep grades, raging waters, and deep chasms, often in conditions that forced the survey parties that moved ahead of the construction crews to travel on horseback.

"It was nothing but Indian trails," General Hoge said in his *Engineer Memoirs.* "Somebody had made a partial air survey of this route. They didn't know where they were going. They had this laid out purely from air photos. . . . There were a lot of places where no one had been. I later got up there and I couldn't even find an Indian (guide) who'd been over parts of it."

Hoge set up a command center for the southern sector in Whitehorse and for the northern sector in Fort St. John. Although he was initially placed in charge of the entire length of the highway, he quickly saw that command, like the construction

Although most did not believe African-American soldiers could perform well in cold climates, the shortage of manpower during World War II forced the U.S. military to send three black regiments to work on the Alaska Highway project. Arriving in Alaska by Greyhound bus *(above)*, these soldiers defied the stereotypes placed upon them and performed at the same level of their white counterparts despite substandard equipment and challenging climate issues.

itself, would need to be broken up into segments. In June 1942, he placed Colonel James A. O'Connor in command of the southern sector.

As construction got under way, the four regiments were joined by the 93rd, 95th, and 97th Regiments, each composed of African-American soldiers commanded by white officers; this brought the total number of troops on the job to more than 11,000. Additional labor would come from civilian workers through the Whitehorse-based Public Roads Administration. By the summer of 1942, 18,000 soldiers and civilians were at work. Harvey Maloney, a member of the first team to survey the route between Fort St. John and Fort Nelson, recalled in the book *The Alaska Highway: A Historic Photographic Journey*, "The engineers blazed a trail for the soldiers to clear and we followed, a day or two behind. Behind us, at first a long way behind, were the bulldozers."

Surveyors were not entirely without help or guideposts along some stretches of the highway. The route passed through lands belonging to the many native groups, or bands, that lived along the route. These members of the First Nations bands—including the Upper Tanana, the Han, and the Ahtna—lived in seasonal camps at Watson Lake and all along the highway corridor in places named Lower Point, Upper Laird, Champagne, Burwash Landing, and Beaver Creek. Yet, none of these groups had the legal power to stop the road from cutting across their land. Indeed, at the time, the United States and Canada did not recognize native land claims.

Along other sections, the locals were hired as guides to help surveyors blaze the route and absorb existing trails into the highway plan. They provided the convoys of mule trains that kept the advance survey teams in supplies and pointed teams toward existing trails and stretches of roads. Like the road from Dawson Creek to Fort St. John, these roads were primarily one-lane dirt paths that would be widened and absorbed into the highway.

There is an old adage that says a journey of 1,000 miles starts with a single step. The building of a highway half that length, however, would require much more work than that.

CHAPTER 2

"Permafrost Was the Worst Thing We Had to Contend With"

Even before the men of the 35th Engineers hit Dawson Creek, preparations for their arrival were under way. Major Alvin Welling—formerly attached to the 35th and now assigned to Colonel Hoge as his executive officer—had arrived in town barely a week before the trains that carried the engineers and soldiers. Having served an earlier tour of duty in Alaska, Major Welling was well aware of the conditions that would face the men, and he knew he had little time to prepare.

Welling's first task was insuring that the people of Dawson Creek and Fort St. John were ready for the massive influx of men and machinery headed their way. He met with town officials and secured their help to line up the necessary railroad sidings, or short stretches of track used to store railcars for unloading; warehouse and other storage facilities; buildings that could be used for headquarters; and fields large enough for troops to set up their tents.

MOVING MEN AND MACHINES

Although Welling met with a local population that was eager and willing to cooperate with him, he worked around the clock for a week. Help finally came the day before the scheduled arrival of the 35th in the form of a detachment of 5 officers and 125 men from the Quartermaster Corps, units that specialized in supplying and provisioning troops. Under their command, this small village with a population of 600 would, literally overnight, explode into a bustling 24-hour-a-day boomtown.

That first night in subarctic Dawson Creek offered the Quartermaster soldiers a taste of the difficulties the engineers and soldiers were soon to face. Unable to drive tent pegs into the frozen ground, they tied down their tents as best they could with ropes, shoveled the snow out from beneath them, and installed portable stoves to provide heat. Instead, the stoves caused the ground to thaw, and the men awoke to find themselves deep in mud.

By the time the first company of the 35th Engineers pulled into town the following day, the weather had started to turn unseasonably warm. Although this was a welcome change for the comfort of the men, warm weather meant an early thaw for the Peace River. The army was relying on several more weeks of cold so that the ice—over which trucks and troops were scheduled to travel—would remain frozen.

Major Welling's solution was to procure all the sawdust and wooden planks he could from local sawmills. The sawdust was spread over the ice as an insulating blanket to protect it from the warming air; the planks were laid on top of that as further insulation and to help spread the weight of the heavy equipment as it crossed the river. The first trucks made the crossing without incident, although not without some anxiety, and reached Fort St. John on the evening of March 11. Their first order of business was to clear a base camp and erect facilities for storing supplies, including the vast quantities of fuel needed to run the trucks, bulldozers, and other construction vehicles.

The slow, steady thaw continued, creating worries that the ice would begin to break before they were finished crossing, thereby destroying any chance of keeping to an already tight schedule. Although the ice was still thick enough to support their equipment, some pieces of which weighed 20 tons or more, each crossing was a cause for concern. The engineers began to wait until the colder nighttime temperatures arrived to send the heaviest pieces across. Still, the ice could be seen sagging and rippling under the weight of the passing vehicles.

Four trains of 35 cars each were required to transport the men of the 35th Engineers to Dawson Creek. One entire train was loaded with enough gasoline, oil, tents, rations, and replacement parts to last the men stationed at Fort Nelson five months. The last of the men of the 35th Engineers reached Dawson Creek on March 16.

Farther up the road, on the route to Fort Nelson, the thaw had already caused problems. The frozen surface—less an actual road than a dirt trail—was melting into a thin layer of muddy slush. For several feet beneath that, the ground remained frozen; however, if the warming trend continued, the way could become impassable. Trucks and heavy machinery would be bogged down in the thick, deep mud.

Colonel Hoge, realizing that the weather endangered his mission, ordered the 35th split into two companies: one that would leave immediately for Fort Nelson along the slowly worsening trail, and another that would wait at Fort St. John. This way, even if the road deteriorated into impassable mud, at least half of his force would be in position to do the work it had been sent to do. Otherwise, the overwhelming number of men and trucks could have clogged the road and practically guaranteed a workforce that was inadequate to the task. To further speed the process of moving all of the necessary equipment and supplies north, Hoge used his truck fleet like a conveyor belt. He sent them from Fort St. John to Fort Nelson, and then back to Dawson Creek, to be reloaded from the supply depots and sent north once again.

The unpredictable climate of the Alaskan wilderness proved to be a great challenge for the highway team. The soldiers, many of whom had never experienced cold climates before, were forced to adapt to the Arctic quickly. *Above,* a crew of soldiers builds a bridge over the White River.

The 250 miles (402 km) between Fort St. John and Fort Nelson were divided into sectors, each with its own temporary base camp. These base camps offered supplies of fuel, a field kitchen serving meals 24 hours a day, heated tents where drivers could rest while fresh drivers replaced them, and a tow truck that was constantly on the move to look for breakdowns or vehicles stuck in the mud.

The march of men and equipment went on day and night. Then, on April 24, the warming trend that had sent temperatures above 50°F (10°C) ended; overnight, the temperature plummeted

80°. The mushy trail froze solid once again. Colonel Hoge immediately scrapped his two-team plan and ordered all units to start moving to Fort Nelson. With no idea whether the freeze would hold, and with the warmer weather of April only days away, they had to take advantage of the freeze while they could. The success of the mission depended on speed and manpower, both of which had been threatened by the temperature and mud.

By the end of March, the warm weather returned, bringing with it the so-called mud season. By then, however, the last of the 35th Engineers and their convoys were on their way north along the steadily worsening trail. At the last minute, a civilian company hired to transport aviation fuel to Fort Nelson found itself ill equipped to deal with the conditions on the trail and pulled out of the job, abandoning hundreds of 55-gallon fuel drums along the route. The Canadian government requested that the army finish the contractors' work. The Quartermaster Corps agreed to the request and, along with the last of the broken-down vehicles that had been left on the side of the trail, brought the fuel drums the rest of the way to Fort Nelson. The last man up the road found that nothing had been left behind by the army but 250 miles (402 km) of mud and tire tracks.

On April 11, 1942, the engineers of the 35th, now safely based at Fort Nelson, were given their orders: "This morning we are going to start the Alcan Highway," the lieutenant in charge of the bulldozers was told. "Take a starting point . . . just west of the Fort Nelson air strip and . . . head west." On April 12, a reporter asked Hoge—who had received a promotion to brigadier general only two weeks earlier—if the route over the Rockies to Whitehorse had been determined. The general replied that he was "strongly encouraged to believe that a favorable route exists through this section (of the mountains)," but he refused to be pinned down, as "the drainage and soil conditions cannot of course be determined until later in the spring." As with many aspects of this unusual project, the army and its engineers had to face each obstacle and challenge as it arose.

Approximately 50 miles (80 km) of foothills lay before the next great obstacle, the eastern slope of the Rocky Mountains. This, they believed, was their greatest challenge. In reality, their biggest problem lay right beneath their feet.

MUSKEG AND PERMAFROST

The 20-ton bulldozers ripped into the treelike west of the Fort Nelson airstrip as ordered, expecting to have an easy job of

BUILDING AMERICA NOW

STUART HIGHWAY: EXPLORING THE OUTBACK

John McDouall Stuart was born in Scotland in 1815 and attended the Scottish Naval and Military Academy, from which he graduated as a civil engineer. He moved to South Australia in 1839. He went into business as a surveyor and, later, operated a farm. Adventuring was in his blood, however, and he joined an 1844 expedition lead by Captain Charles Sturt. The expedition's goal was to determine the geographic center of the Australian continent and settle, once and for all, the long-debated question of whether or not there was an inland sea at the heart of this largely unexplored land whose cities and settlements were located primarily along the coastal areas.

Captain Sturt had earlier attempted expeditions into the mysterious Outback. In 1840, he followed the Murray River, which flowed west, apparently into Australia's interior, but his 1,000-mile (1,600 km) journey led him to nothing more than a large, stagnant lake on the South Australian coastline. Numerous expeditions throughout the early part of the century resulted in failure and death.

Stuart would undertake several expeditions of his own into the heart of Australia during the 1840s and 1850s. He searched not only clearing a swath through the wilderness. Yet, after knocking down the first few hundred yards of trees and shoveling them aside, the engineers discovered an unanticipated problem: mud.

The bulldozer's great tracks quickly stirred up the soft clay silt, or super-fine soil, which turns into a thick, gooey mud when mixed with water. Commanders ordered their men to keep going, to push through the muck; they believed that exposure to the warm spring winds and sun would dry the mud and get rid of

for the fabled inland sea but for valuable mineral deposits and for farming and grazing lands as well. Australia's hostile Outback bested Stuart until his 1861–1862 expedition, which set out from Adelaide in South Australia. Though he faced disease, hostile Aborigines, and temperatures that could reach 120°F (49°C), he succeeded in reaching the northern coast, near present-day Darwin. More important, he survived the journey—if only just barely. He had to be carried home on a stretcher for the difficult trek back to Adelaide.

Stuart's efforts not only proved that Australia's interior was home to desert and that no inland sea existed, it also opened the way to the continent's Northern Territory and defined the route that Charles Todd, the postmaster general of South Australia, would follow in 1872, with few deviations, to lay the Overland Telegraph. The route of the Overland Telegraph linked the far ends of the continent via a single 1,988-mile (3,200 km) galvanized iron wire strung along 36,000 poles, and, ultimately, on to England by underwater cable via already existing lines at Java, Indonesia, approximately 1,000 miles to the east. The telegraph line would lead to the establishment of towns along its length, the building of a railroad, and, more than a century later, a highway named for the man who first penetrated the interior.

the wet conditions. April rains and the runoff from the melting snows were more than enough to offset the drying effects of the sun, however. The ground remained a dense, muddy mess that kept progress at a literal crawl.

The muck also damaged the equipment. Vehicles routinely suffered from damaged axles and transmissions; at one point, the engineers had only four functioning trucks while they awaited the arrival of spare parts. By April 30, almost three weeks after the official start of construction, only 8 miles (13 km) of road had been cleared.

The first anyone heard of muskeg [a swamp or bog formed by thousands of years of accumulated decayed vegetative matter common to glacial regions] was when the troops arrived in Alaska and began their work. No one knew what to make of the warnings by the locals of the conditions that lay ahead. On PBS's "Building the Alaska Highway," army engineer Chester Russell recalled with amusement one such warning received by his sergeant: "This fella told Sergeant King, 'You better watch that muskeg because it'll get you.' Sergeant King, he was patting his old .45 (handgun), and he says, "That's all right, I've got my .45. I'm not afraid of it.' We learned what muskeg was for sure, I'll guarantee you."

During the winter, the frozen muskeg is hard and can be driven on, but once it begins to thaw, said civil engineer Billy Connor on "Building the Alaska Highway," "you end up with a large shallow lake. Think of thawing muskeg as a big sponge. If you put weight on it, the water squishes out and everything sinks, and you end up having a very difficult time getting across that terrain."

Some stretches of muskeg were several miles long and could extend as far as 25 feet (7.6 m) deep. Engineers used dynamite and bulldozers to clear larger sections of this troublesome goo, but some muskeg pools could literally swallow a bulldozer. Whenever a stretch that bad was encountered, the engineers would go around the problem. Troubling as that was, muskeg ranked

The route of the Alaska Highway cut through mountain ranges and forests. Although clearing the forests was expected to be an easy task, the equipment and men were soon bogged down in mud. *Above*, a Caterpillar tractor widens the roadway.

a distant second to permafrost, the permanent layer of frozen ground (at varying depths beneath the muskeg) that had stayed at below-freezing temperatures continuously for anywhere from a few years to several thousand years.

"Everyone talked of muskeg and everybody talked of mountains and crossing lakes and rivers," recalled General Hoge, "but they had never heard of permafrost, which was the worst thing we had to contend with."

In the early winter days of construction, bulldozers would clear a stretch of highway anywhere from 60 to 90 feet (18.28 to 27.43 m) wide of muskeg, trees, roots, and rocks by literally scraping them from the surface and pushing them off to the side. While temperatures remained below freezing, these roadbeds were solid and passable; indeed, at Arctic temperatures of −30° to −60°F (−34.4°C to −51.1°C), whatever the bulldozers exposed to the sun—whether it was dirt or solid ice—remained as hard as rock. The exposed roadbed was then allowed to dry in the sun as workers moved on, leaving it to trailing work crews to add polish to the pioneer road. They would widen, straighten, and grade the crude paths, using the timber felled by axes and bulldozers as the raw material with which to construct the road and build culverts and bridges. This technique worked fine in most areas.

Yet, engineers and builders unfamiliar with the Arctic phenomenon of permafrost found that, rather than solve the water problem, the warming rays of the sun only made matters worse by melting the top several inches of the long-covered ice. The temperature of permafrost is approximately 30°F (−1.1°C); the freezing point of water is 32°F (0°C), so a rise of as little as 3° is enough to cause melting. The trouble came with the onset of the warming spring weather. The melting ice saturated the surrounding soil, turning the freshly cut swath of road into a bed of impassable mud and muck. "(If) you couldn't go on, you moved right or left, one or the other. You moved," said army engineer Wallace Lytle on "Building the Alaska Highway."

Speed was everything. "The water and slush ran at times 4 or 5 inches (10–12 centimeters) over the running boards of the International truck I was riding in," said truck driver Ray Haman in *The Alaska Highway*. The scrape-and-dry method "was absolutely wrong with permafrost," said General Hoge. "You had to do it exactly the reverse. You had to save all (the muskeg) and put it right back on, cover it over with dirt. I didn't have gravel, but (muskeg) made a blanket that protected (the permafrost)."

The first permafrost was encountered early on, along the road north to Whitehorse. It did not reoccur until almost 725 miles (1,166 km) farther north, when it was found again near Kluane Lake. The 18th Combat Regiment Engineers had been making record time northward from Whitehorse—according to General Hoge, "more mileage than I'd ever made"—when the problem was discovered.

Gravel is often used as material to fill wet areas because it allows water to drain away from the surface quickly, but it was not available to these fast-moving workers in remote wilderness areas. Engineers tried installing ditches to drain the melting waters, but these could not handle the steady flow.

Where once engineers had averaged 400 miles (741 km) of road a month, progress was reduced to a crawl. Six weeks of trial and error were required before they hit upon the solution to the problem of permafrost. Yet, as civil engineer Billy Connor was quick to point out, "The Army engineers were problem solvers. In combat you have to come up with a solution to whatever problem you're facing very quickly and efficiently in order to move the war effort forward. They had not known about permafrost, but they were able to adapt what they knew to the problem at hand."

They might have been adaptable, but the problem nonetheless slowed construction down to 1 mile (1.5 km) of road a day. The builders learned the hard way that all that stood between them and a hopeless quagmire was a thin layer of rotting vegetation. The bulldozers were left behind, and the highway's approximately 100-foot-wide (30 m) corridor was cut by hand instead. Leaving the protective layer of muskeg in place, the roadbed was then built up with logs laid tightly together to form a corduroy road (named for the rough texture of corduroy fabric). One 32-mile (51 km) stretch of highway through the permafrost south of the Donjek River—which was little more than a winter trail through the wilderness when it was done—took six weeks of round-the-clock labor to complete.

Accidents were not uncommon during construction. Hundreds of men worked with powerful and dangerous machinery in treacherous conditions. Vehicles often went off the road or overturned, and the heavy machinery often slipped in the mud and ice. Overcrowding also presented dangers. In February 1943, a fire broke out in Dawson Creek, which now was inhabited by more than 20,000 people. A warehouse in the overcrowded downtown caught fire, and the fire spread to neighboring warehouses, barns, and stables, including one where a truck loaded with dynamite

THE TRAGEDY AT CHARLIE LAKE

Permafrost wasn't the only water-related obstacle unique to extreme northern construction. In fact, before they even arrived at the job site, the crews had to deal with ice—or rather the *absence* of it. The members of the 35th Engineers who arrived by rail at Dawson Creek in March 1942 were sent the 50 miles (80 km) to Fort Nelson along a narrow farm road with a full complement of supplies, including heavy trucks and earth-moving equipment.

After the Peace River had thawed but before the first timber trestle bridge across the river was completed in October (it stood only one month before being swept away by high water), the army pressed ferries into service. The supply routes to the fast-moving crews were all-important and never ending; in all, some 250,000 tons of supplies would be used to feed, clothe, shelter, and equip the soldiers along the 1,500 miles (2,414 km) of the highway. Troops did what was necessary to get from point A to point B as fast as they could, as was the case on May 15, 1942, at Charlie Lake, just north of Fort St. John.

Having reached the shores of the lake, the 341st Engineers assembled a raft out of two pontoons, or flotation devices, and a section of prefabricated road. Onto this was loaded a weapons carrier, a D-4 Caterpillar tractor, food supplies, and men to be transported the 9 miles (14 km) down Charlie Lake to the next position. A sudden storm blew in and caused the tractor to slide, capsizing the makeshift barge in the heavy waves of the squall. A local trapper braved three trips in his small boat to rescue the five survivors who clung to the wreckage. In all, twelve men drowned in the freezing waters.

was parked. Five people were killed in the explosion, more than 100 were injured, and an entire city block was destroyed.

ICE, WATER, AND MUD

Water was a dangerous obstacle all along the route of the Alaska Highway. Because working conditions would have been too harsh in the winter months—and because construction had to be done quickly—the grueling work of hacking a highway out of the wilderness would take place in the spring and summer months. Spring, however, was when the previous winter's accumulated snow and ice melted into running water.

Big floods meant big problems for engineers attempting to carve a road out of the lowest, most level stretch of ground available. "(The water) came off the mountains and ran off all sorts of ways," recalled General Hoge in his memoirs. "Part of it emptied into the Columbia (River), part of it emptied into the Yukon (River), and part of it went on down I think into the Mississippi. . . . You had big floods."

Fort Nelson, where construction began, was a trading post that consisted of five log buildings on the bend of the Fort Nelson River. It had a reputation as "one of the loneliest and most isolated trading posts in the entire Northwest," according to contemporary reports. It also had a history of flooding, which destroyed the post in 1890. It was rebuilt on higher ground.

When the crews first arrived to start work on the highway, they faced solid ice and ground so hard it might as well have been steel. All along the route, the melting ice and thawing ground presented challenges. Drainage ditches and culverts, or drainage pipe used to divert surface water under a roadway or other obstruction, were laid as needed. The crews, who were often forced to work ahead of the supply chain, often improvised because the needed supplies were not available due to wartime shortages. If there were no pipes to lay, they used wooden boxes and old oil drums; one of the most common types of improvised

Seasonal thaws created mud pits in areas with permafrost and muskeg. Confronted with building on these unstable surfaces, the army's Corps of Engineers advised the soldiers to construct corduroy roads and dig drainage ditches. These inventive solutions allowed work to continue, but progress on the roadway slowed as trucks and bulldozers became stuck and damaged.

culverts was made of wooden staves, or narrow strips of wood held together by metal straps, like a barrel.

Yet, there was little that men and machines could do in the face of nature. The land did what it had done since it had been formed. The U.S. Army's attempts to tame nature were only partially successful, but these engineers were nothing if not adaptable.

North of Whitehorse was a stretch of road known as the "Grand Canyon of the Alaska Highway," a narrow ditch formed by the gradually draining and settling silt. The constant flow of heavy trucks and construction equipment that passed over this unstable area only hastened the settling. This part of the road was often closed for days at a time due to impassable conditions.

Another section of highway almost 40 miles (64 km) between Pickhandle Lake and Beaver Creek was first blazed and cut in the winter of 1942. By spring, however, rushing water had erased any trace of the builders' efforts. That section of road remained impassable until October 1943.

Troops often improvised rafts that allowed them to be towed by bulldozers and trucks over the knee-deep mud that filled the road. Floods would submerge trucks almost to their roofs and strand heavy equipment in muck that overwhelmed their tracks. "The ground was so soft that one truck could not follow in another's tracks without bogging down," recalled one worker in *The Alaska Highway: A Historic Photographic Journey.* "Each driver took his best shot and kept going as long as he could. Sometimes you would see a (truck) hauling a 'train' of three or four trucks, dragging them through the (mud). Our one-and-a-half ton (trucks) were too light for the going and many springs and axles were broke."

"We had some practice in road building at Fort Bragg," Master Sergeant George H. Burke of the 95th Engineers told the author of *The Alaska Highway,* "but we were held up for weeks by heavy rains and we began to think that we would never make the first four miles because we couldn't get our drainage work done." Yet, as difficult as those first miles were, they were only a taste of what lay ahead for the builders of the Alaska Highway.

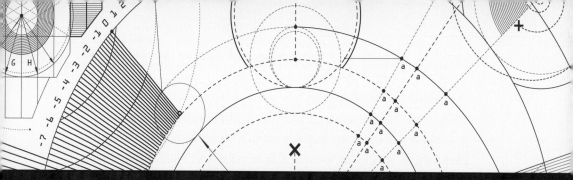

CHAPTER 3

"When One Company Finished Their Work, They Would Leapfrog Ahead"

"It looked like we didn't know what we were doing," said army engineer Bill Batey on "Building the Alaska Highway." "Sometimes we'd head off one way and head off another way, and finally end up going through the most favorable route, not the best, but the most favorable."

On-the-spot improvisation was required for most of the length of the road to Alaska via Canada, popularly known as the Alcan Highway. From the actual route to the methods for carving relatively level and, hopefully, sustainable surfaces out of whatever conditions happened to greet the engineers along the way, the highway was not a project whose problems could be foreseen.

The fastest and easiest way to locate routes through deep forests, along rocky ledges, and over unstable landscapes was by air. As difficult as the initial miles had proven for the engineers and men not yet familiar with subarctic working conditions and challenges, their hard-won experience and the warming weather began to improve their progress. Yet by June, after three months of often frustrating work, only 360 miles (579 km) of road had been finished. That left six months in which to lay almost three times that many miles, many of them over the Rocky Mountains.

UP IN THE AIR

To build a road that provided access to these remote places, surveyors and engineers first had to get to them. Although conditions on the ground could be examined by teams on horseback, the determination of the big picture of the terrain ahead depended on air travel. Satellites did not yet exist to give digital views of the Canadian and Alaskan landscape; instead, the workers had to rely on slow-moving aircraft and cameras or, just as likely, the naked eye.

By far the greatest challenge for the Alcan was getting across the Rockies. Numerous passes at varying altitudes were suggested, evaluated, and discarded. The higher the road climbed, the steeper and more difficult it was to navigate. Another disadvantage to a route at higher altitudes was the weather, which grew colder the higher one climbed.

General Hoge had his pilot fly him over the proposed pass that would take the road down to the Yukon River. "The place they had mapped out for me . . . was up above the timber line and was in the snow country," he recounted in his *Engineer Memoirs*. "It would have been one hell of a job to get up there and then get down. . . . They just picked (the route) off of a map someplace, an airplane map or something. They had no information. They had a few (aerial) photographs . . . but that was all they knew about it."

Like the engineers and surveyors who often hired natives as guides through the wilderness, General Hoge relied on a local to be his expert guide to the country—in this case, bush pilot Les Cook. He called Cook a "crackerjack" pilot and credited him as "the one that showed me the route to follow." Cook and men like him were vital to the success of the highway project. They provided the only reliable form of transportation up and down the narrow corridor and over the Rockies. "Les took me everyplace. He went between the mountains. We went down at elevations. We got lost, but I got to know the country pretty well." A local trapper who often flew with Cook recalled that he was a man who could be trusted to know where and when to fly, telling his passengers, "My neck's just as important to me as yours is to you."

Even experienced army aviators could not be expected to quickly master the peculiarities of the local flying conditions. Sometimes, especially when crossing the mountains, there was little room for error. "If you could get your foot out of the door, you could touch the top of the trees," General Hoge said. "Those were hair-raising experiences."

Pilots unfamiliar with these conditions were at a disadvantage. Two squadrons of army air force fighters and bombers

Without roads or infrastructure, the most efficient form of transportation within the Alaskan wilderness was the airplane. General Hoge and his staff were heavily dependent on experienced bush pilots like Les Cook (above), who had flown Hoge over the entire route of the proposed highway.

sent to Alaska to bolster defenses against a possible Japanese invasion and help ferry supplies around the northwest territories proved the difficulties of flying under these conditions. "The airfields were in a very primitive state of construction and not all of them were operational," historian Heath Twichell said in "Building the Alaska Highway." "The combination of lack of navigation aids, untrained pilots, bad weather, and bad luck resulted in most of those planes crashing before they got to Alaska. It was a real fiasco."

Pilots like Cook were based out of tiny airfields that dotted the countryside, many of which were no more than a dirt runway, a wind sock, and a hut. In some places, local residents would scrape out an airfield by hand, as the Athapaskan Band did in Tanacross, Alaska, in 1935. Grant McConachie built many other airfields during the 1930s for use by the airplanes of his Yukon Southern Air Transport company. He built one in Watson Lake in 1939. In 1941, the army took over that crude little airstrip and expanded it into a 5,000-foot (1,524 m) paved landing strip with cleared landing approaches. The army took over similar small airstrips along the route, enlarging and paving some to accommodate the steady flow of workers and material that were necessary to keep the highway construction project moving.

AERIAL OBSERVATIONS AND NARROW GAGES

General Hoge and his surveyors, at first unfamiliar with the terrain over which they were building the road, quickly learned the lay of the land. This was due, in large part, to all of the flying back and forth that they were forced to endure. "I learned much about this country and where to go," General Hoge said. "I also learned from the air that I could distinguish the type of soil from the type of timber on it. . . . For instance, cedar always grew on gravelly soil . . . when you saw spruce that was usually mucky, and it was soft soil. . . . Poplar and birch always grew in sandy soil."

"IT WAS SUPPOSED TO BE A SECRET MISSION"

Even with the massive movement of men and material that would soon be traveling north by sea and rail, the Alaska Highway was supposed to be a secret operation. As a wartime emergency construction project in a remote area, separated from enemy forces by only 750 miles (1,207 km), the highway was considered vulnerable to sabotage. Although discretion was the government's intent, the reality of keeping a 1,600-plus-mile (2,575 km) highway a secret through inhabited—if often only barely—regions was another matter entirely.

In the summer of 1942, Arthur Northwood Jr., a reporter for *Time* magazine, arrived in Alaska. "I had no instructions on civilians who came up there," General Hoge later recalled. "I showed him around a little bit, what was going on, talked to him. I didn't give him any secrets or anything else." Yet after the article "Barracks with Bath" was published in the August 31, 1942, issue of the news weekly, "the War Department called me up. They wanted to stop this business. It was supposed to be a secret mission, but I had no ability to keep people out of the territory. They came up into Canadian territory, and they had a passport and they had a perfect right to be there."

Even earlier, in February, when Hoge had gone to Edmonton to brief Canadian officials on his mission, secrecy had been difficult to maintain. Reporters in the provincial capital had not failed to take note of the colonel and his traveling companions. "After all," wrote historian Heath Twichell in "Northwest Epic," "how many plausible explanations could there be for the appearance of four high-ranking American officials, three of them road-building experts, in western Canada?"

Several days later, on February 19, an article appeared in the *Ottawa Journal* to the effect that the U.S. military was studying the feasibility of "the proposed route" for a highway that was to run through "Fort St. John, Fort Nelson, Whitehorse and into Alaska."

Once more, it was a local who offered the inexperienced construction effort its best advice: Canadian Herb Wheeler, chairman of the board of the White Pass and Yukon Railroad. In addition to running the railroad, Wheeler had also built roads as well as airports at Skagway and Whitehorse, and he had once run a stagecoach line from Dawson up the Yukon River. "He gave me more good information on the type of country and the way of construction than anybody I ran into," the general said.

The White Pass and Yukon Railroad was an enormously important link in the construction effort. The line ran 110 miles (177 km) northward from Skagway, Alaska, to Whitehorse in the Yukon. Skagway was then a tiny port town with a population of less than 1,000 located at the head of the Taiya Inlet, off the Gulf of Alaska. The railroad had been constructed at the end of the Klondike gold rush, following the 1896 discovery of gold by members of the Tagish Band in the Yukon.

The track was laid by hand on a bed hacked through some of the continent's most rugged territory. Because it had to pass through such harsh conditions, the railroad was built at the narrow gauge (the width between the tracks) of 36 inches (91.5 cm) rather than the standard 56.5 inches (143.5 cm). When the U.S. government leased the line for the duration of the war, they simply used what they had. The 770th Railway Operating Battalion took over operation in October 1942, upgrading the 40-plus-year-old line and locating working engines and railcars that could run on the narrow track. Engines had to be shipped in from the lower 48 states or diverted from delivery to the railroads of other nations. In one instance, an original engine that had run to the gold fields was refurbished and pressed into service.

The railroad's rolling stock would eventually number three-dozen engines and almost 300 freight cars. During 1943 alone, the White Pass and Yukon Railway moved more than 280,000 tons of supplies along its length. Almost overnight, Skagway changed from a remote settlement to a thriving boomtown nearly bursting at the seams, like dozens of towns along the highway route, with thousands of troops.

ACROSS THE GREAT DIVIDE

Thanks to a Watson Lake native and a Public Roads Administration (PRA) employee, the pass through the Rockies was finally located ahead of the approaching construction workers. The McCusker Trail was a steep, winding trail pioneered in 1898 that wound through the Liard River Valley, reaching its highest point near Summit Lake at an elevation of 4,250 feet (1,295 m), before snaking down through the narrow Sentinel and Barricade mountain range gorges and then on to Watson Lake. The army scouting teams had made numerous flights over the trail but thought it was likely unsuitable for their needs. Construction over this route—though possible—could not, they determined, be accomplished in the single, short season in which they had to finish their work. The trail was impassable in winter because of the deep snows and during spring and summer because of the muskeg.

Other problems existed as well, including the same silt-like soil that had slowed the engineers at the start of the road west of Fort Nelson. Additionally, the Liard River was too wide and ran too swiftly at a necessary crossing point. The military's earliest aerial surveys of the trail had convinced them that the problems were too numerous and difficult to make the route practical. Still, the area offered little in the way of alternatives.

A PRA employee who had recently traveled the McCusker Trail by dogsled told the scouts that the winding trail was, in fact, perfect for their needs. Despite its daunting appearance, he believed that, with modern road-building techniques and equipment at their disposal, the highway could go through there with relative ease.

A native of Watson Lake was approached and asked how *he* would travel from the lake to Fort Nelson. The man responded that there was only one way, and that was by the McCusker Trail.

A railroad connecting Whitehorse and Skagway became an invaluable means of delivering supplies and materials to the Alaska Highway project. *Above,* trains carry supplies to the men working on the Alaska Highway.

The man suggested a possible but dubious alternative: down the Liard River, then up the Trout River to Muncho Lake. He added, "Not sure though. Nobody ever go that way."

Following the Watson Lake man's directions from the air, the engineers were surprised and delighted to find that the suggested route was exactly what they had been looking for. The route offered only one obstacle: A sheer limestone cliff blocked the route on the eastern shore of Muncho Lake. This could be overcome, however, with enough dynamite to carve a ledge out of the cliff for the roadway.

Back at Fort Nelson, the engineers' report was greeted with relief. The route was approved in early May. The last major hurdle to the road, the formidable Rocky Mountains, seemed to have been cleared. Interestingly, General Hoge had been shown this very same route from the air by bush pilot Les Cook almost two months earlier. This had set Hoge's mind at ease about where the mountains could be crossed, even if it would take this later mission to confirm it.

Although obstacles like permafrost and the cliffs of Summit Lake slowed some crews, others made far better time. The job of clearing and laying the road became routine; the workers

BUILDING AMERICA NOW

STUART HIGHWAY: THE TRACK

The stringing of the Overland Telegraph required the establishment of relay, or repeater, stations (locations where the electrical signal traveling along the telegraph wire is boosted, or strengthened, enabling it to continue its journey) along its length. These stations also served to help maintain the telegraph wire, which could break, and the 3,600 poles it was strung along, which could be toppled or washed away by heavy rains and floods.

All of these stations were manned and had to be kept supplied. The route that linked them came to be known simply as "the Track." Most of these stations never evolved into anything more than outposts along the way, but many would grow into the towns and cities that now flourish along the modern-day Stuart Highway. These outposts were settled by farmers, ranchers, and miners (gold and other valuable minerals had been discovered as early as 1850 in Victoria); laborers who dug postholes for the telegraph's poles discovered gold at Yam Creek in 1870.

averaged, according to General Hoge, 14 miles (22 km) a day. "We had a task force ahead which was clearing with big bulldozers and small manpower," he recalled. "Then they were followed by the first company who cleared, cleared the timber away and got something prepared. Then they put in some culverts, and they were followed by other companies. When one of them had completed its section, it would then leapfrog forward, so that when you finished a section, that company picked up and went to the head of the column and passed on ahead."

The engineers had determined that this leapfrog approach was the best technique for building a road of this length. If the entire

For most of the nineteenth century and into the first half of the twentieth century, the Track remained the only lifeline between these remote outposts and the rest of civilization. In the days before refrigeration, meat had to be provided "on the hoof," or delivered live to be slaughtered and consumed as needed. Alfred Giles, who had worked to build the Overland Telegraph line, changed occupations and became a supplier of fresh meat. On his first trip up the Track, he drove 7,000 sheep from South Australia to the stations in the Northern Territory, a journey that took him an entire year to complete.

In 1889, the Palmerston and Pine Creek Railway line, which followed the general route of the Track, was opened in the Northern Territory. Over the years, it would be extended south to Katherine and, by 1929, to Birdum. The Pine Creek line was shut down in 1976. Although a north-to-south rail line had long been discussed, it was not until February 2004 that a rail line from Adelaide in the south to Darwin in the north was finally completed. It would, however, take the outbreak of World War II to turn the dusty old Track into something that more closely resembled a real road.

workforce had set to work at one end of the road and moved forward, workers would always be waiting for those ahead of them to complete their jobs before they could do their own.

With six regiments at his disposal, General Hoge split the road into six sections. The 35th Engineers were the first in, traveling over the ice to Fort Nelson to build the 360 miles (579 km) of road north to Watson Lake. They carried their own supplies with them. "They lived on C-rations for about three months," General Hoge said of the isolated regiment. "That was all they had . . . vegetable hash, meat hash, and chile con carne. Sometimes they had chili for breakfast and sometimes they had it for dinner, but they always had three choices." For most of the spring, the 35th cut its way through the Canadian wilderness, remaining in isolation until it joined up with the 341st General Service Regiment coming up from the south with its section of the highway, the 260 miles (418 km) from Fort St. John to Fort Nelson.

The 340th started construction on a 200-mile (321 km) stretch of a branch highway that would connect coastal Morley Bay (now called Nisutlin Bay) on Teslin Lake with the main road farther inland (near Champagne) that was being laid by the northward-working 35th from Fort Nelson. To supply the fast-moving troops, engineers of the 93rd were assigned to cut a 70-mile (112 km) access road east from the Carcross Station on the White Pass and Yukon Railroad to Teslin Lake.

SUPPLY CHAINS

The steady, reliable stream of supplies and equipment was vital to the speedy completion of the pioneer road through the wilderness. Without the access road to Teslin Lake, the only method of moving supplies in the summer months was by steamboat and barge up the Yukon River.

In fact, the equipment that the 93rd needed to build the access road was stuck on the docks in Seattle, Washington. The troops were forced to start work with hand tools. As with most challenges along the highway, they completed their task with the

Truck shipments from Edmonton, Canada, would travel over the Mackenzie River *(above)* to replenish the supplies at Dawson Creek. The food and equipment that was delivered to the southern work site of the Alaska Highway project was shared with Canadian oil pipeline employees. Soldiers in the north received their materials by way of the Yukon Railroad.

tools they had. By June 18, 1942, the access road was cut and the engineers of the 340th were able to start their push north to Watson Lake.

Supplies that came in on the White Pass and Yukon Railroad were trucked to centrally located Whitehorse. As construction progressed, supplies began to move up the road behind the workers. The military was sharing resources with the civilian contractors of the PRA, who followed behind the army engineers, and with those who worked on an oil pipeline and access road for CANOL (Canadian Oil). "All of our food, all of . . . the materials, and the equipment for these contractors had to come over that railroad, in addition to whatever supplies we were getting," said General Hoge. "(The train) only made one run a day, so it was congested and was very difficult to get anything up there, so we were very limited on the supplies we could get in to build anything."

At the southern end of the highway, Dawson Creek was the major supply point. Alaska's existing highways and railroad lines that linked Anchorage on the Gulf of Alaska with Fairbanks—about 400 miles (643 km) inland—were also used to move material and supplies. Riverboats and barges floated heavy equipment and supplies to points along the route, and other craft were moved on the Mackenzie River down from Edmonton, Alberta.

Soon enough, however, the difficulty was less getting supplies *to* a location than it was getting them at all. "When we got started, everything was fine," General Hoge said in his *Engineer Memoirs*. "We were number one (in priority to receive equipment and supplies), but as soon as we got started, we became way back down the line. We became number six or eight in priority."

Even when supply ships did arrive, they did not always bring what was needed. This was the case with one shipment, which bore nothing more than 90 tons of Coca-Cola and beer and several hundred tons of coal and wood for fuel. Although the beverages might have been welcome by those thirsting for a little taste of home, the coal and wood were useless to men who had been issued *oil*-burning stoves.

To rectify the problem, General Hoge made several trips back to Washington, D.C., to plead his case for an uninterrupted chain of supplies. With the war going on, however, many projects were competing for the same resources and limited equipment.

One such rival for supplies was the CANOL Pipeline. Connecting Whitehorse with the oil fields 500 miles (804 km) north at Norman Wells, the pipeline was another vital link in the

North American defense strategy; it briefly paralleled and kept the Alaska Highway corridor supplied with a steady flow of oil. "CANOL took priority for a while," General Hoge said. "They would get all of our equipment. We were already up there. We would starve to death if we didn't keep going."

General Hoge knew he could not allow interruptions in the supply chain to slow construction. If the necessary machinery was not available to do a job, that job still got done with hand tools and manual labor. "We had to make speed and all I was trying to do was to get this road behind me. My specifications . . . were to supply the troops that were ahead . . . with food and fuel and all the repair parts, which was a job in itself; but that made a road."

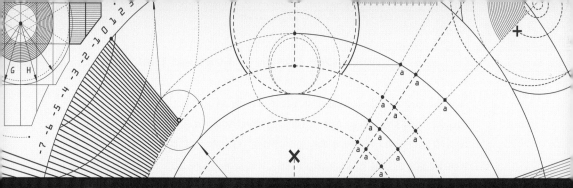

CHAPTER 4

"This Is No Picnic"

Workers who applied for jobs with civilian contractors Bechtel-Price Callahan for the CANOL pipeline project were greeted by the following sign at the hiring halls where they gathered:

> This is No Picnic! Working and living conditions on this job are as difficult as those encountered on any construction job in the United States or foreign territory. Men hired for this job will be required to work and live under the most extreme conditions imaginable. Temperatures will range from 90 above zero to 70 below zero. Men will have to fight swamps, rivers, ice and cold. Mosquitos [sic], flies and gnats will not only be annoying but will cause bodily harm. If you are not prepared to work under these and similar conditions, DO NOT APPLY.

This warning was a brutally frank assessment of what conditions would be like on the CANOL project. The same held true for the soldiers who built the highway.

CANOL PIPELINE

During construction, Whitehorse remained the main supply point for the entire project. The materials, which arrived by ship and then rail via the White Pass and Yukon Railway, were trucked along the Richardson Highway. From there, they could be sent up the road as needed.

Norman Wells, located about 500 miles (804 km) up the Mackenzie River from Whitehorse, was home to a little-known, undeveloped Canadian oil field. The army decided to develop these oil resources as a backup in the event of a Japanese attack that might cut off oil supplies from the south. The oil was to be piped to the refinery at Whitehorse through the 4-inch (10 cm) CANOL pipeline, where it would be processed in the new refinery before it was shipped up the highway route to keep the bulldozers, the jeeps, and the rest of the construction effort moving.

Before the pipeline could be laid, however, docks, cargo-handling facilities, and a road had to be built. Men were also needed to operate the barges and pontoon rafts that would ferry supplies for CANOL. The grueling job of constructing the CANOL road in some of the most brutal conditions experienced by any workers on the project was assigned to the men of the African-American 388th Engineer Battalion. At that time, the military was segregated, which meant that white troops and black troops were kept in separate units and were not allowed to mingle—a practice that would be ended by President Harry S. Truman in 1948. Civilian workers hired by the contracting firm of Bechtel-Price Callahan to work on the road and refinery could choose whether or not they wished to labor under these conditions; the African-American soldiers could not.

Along with two pontoon battalions of white soldiers, the 388th were shipped north to Waterways to construct the CANOL road. They also supported what would grow into a 1,200-mile (1,931 km) supply system that would stretch across both land and water, including Lake Athabasca and the Great Slave Lake, down to the Mackenzie River. The CANOL road connected with

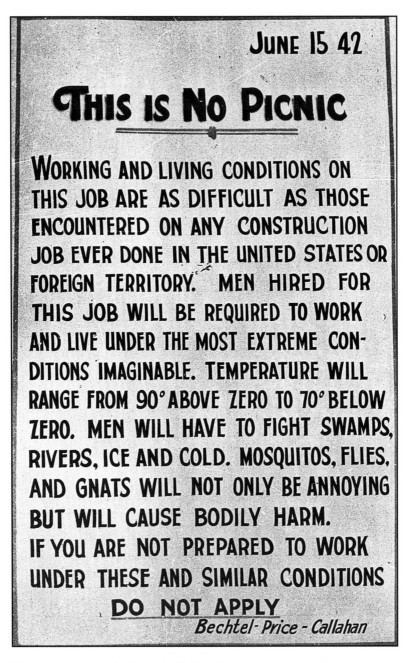

JUNE 15 42

THIS IS NO PICNIC

WORKING AND LIVING CONDITIONS ON THIS JOB ARE AS DIFFICULT AS THOSE ENCOUNTERED ON ANY CONSTRUCTION JOB EVER DONE IN THE UNITED STATES OR FOREIGN TERRITORY. MEN HIRED FOR THIS JOB WILL BE REQUIRED TO WORK AND LIVE UNDER THE MOST EXTREME CONDITIONS IMAGINABLE. TEMPERATURE WILL RANGE FROM 90° ABOVE ZERO TO 70° BELOW ZERO. MEN WILL HAVE TO FIGHT SWAMPS, RIVERS, ICE AND COLD. MOSQUITOS, FLIES, AND GNATS WILL NOT ONLY BE ANNOYING BUT WILL CAUSE BODILY HARM.
IF YOU ARE NOT PREPARED TO WORK UNDER THESE AND SIMILAR CONDITIONS DO NOT APPLY

Bechtel-Price-Callahan

Recruiters placed signs in their offices warning potential applicants of the brutal working conditions at the work sites *(above)*.

the main highway at Johnson's Crossing, approximately midway along the Alcan Highway.

The white engineers were assigned the tasks of building docks and cargo facilities at Norman Wells, as well as the operation of the barges and ferries. The black troops were responsible for the heavy lifting, for building the road and assisting on the construction of the pipeline through the harsh terrain, and for unloading and reloading up to 300 tons of supplies a day, including the endless miles of pipe that would carry the oil to and from the refinery.

In terms of supplies, the CANOL project was given priority over even the road itself. Yet, as was the case with the entire highway, General Hoge was determined to forge ahead and get the job done with the supplies and resources on hand. "But the specifications for our road were that (we) had to supply the troops, and (we) had to have a decent road to get food, gasoline, and equipment up to the troops that were working," the general said in his memoirs. As for the CANOL road itself, that work was left mainly to the civilian contractors, although Hoge "tested the turns, the radius on curves and what not, till I was sure that I could get our trucks and so on around them." Ultimately, the final say on even that part of the operation was left to the efficient General Hoge.

In all, the CANOL road, the pipeline between Norman Wells and Whitehorse, and the refinery would cost approximately $134 million. Soon after the end of the war, the entire project would be abandoned and the refinery dismantled.

BRIDGING THE WATERS

At the start of the Alaska Highway project in the winter of 1942, the problem of crossing large bodies of water with thousands of men, convoys of vehicles, and tons of equipment had a single, simple answer: ice. The frozen lakes, ponds, streams, and rivers encountered along the route were still frozen and, therefore, relatively simple to cross.

Even as spring and warmer weather began to set in, crossings were still possible, as was the case with the Peace River. Tons of sawdust and wooden planks had been spread over the ice to protect it long enough for the convoys to make it across.

Soon enough, however, the ice lost its battle to spring and melted. Barges and ferries replaced the trucks that crossed the winter ice over lakes and larger rivers. Aircraft were also used to move men and equipment. Because of all the rivers and lakes

BUILDING AMERICA NOW

STUART HIGHWAY: WARTIME EMERGENCY

Australia is known as the land down under. Although it seems to be far away, on the other side of the earth in the Southern Hemisphere, the distance between the northern edge of the continent and the southern end of the Japanese island chain is less than 4,000 miles (6,400 km). Australia was no less vulnerable to Japanese attack than was the Alaska territory to Japan's north. Darwin, on the northern shore of Australia, was home to the country's vast oil storage facilities as well as a naval base on the Indian Ocean to keep offshore waters secure. (When the Japanese did attack the Australian oil facilities, however, they did so by air rather than by sea. In February, March, and June of 1942, they succeeded in the almost total destruction of Australia's oil reserves at Darwin.)

The Northern Territory was suddenly of vital strategic importance. Keeping it safe from attack—and supplied from the south in the event of sustained fighting—meant maintaining an open road between the north and the more heavily industrialized south. Similar to the situation in the Alaska territory, that meant the implementation of an emergency road construction program.

along the highway route, pontoon planes—aircraft that could land and take off from the water and did not require traditional airfields—were popular.

The route of the Alaska Highway crossed thousands of small streams and major rivers in its run from Dawson Creek to Fairbanks. By the time the first rough road was finished, it would feature 133 bridges and 8,000 culverts that spanned everything from minor springs and streams to major rivers. Some of these

Like the Alaska Highway, there was no time for niceties. No one expected the Track to be transformed from dirt path to paved highway overnight, or even in the course of a year. Instead, the builders would have to be content to widen, straighten, and otherwise improve the dirt highway running through a wide variety of climatic conditions the length of the continent. They could also seal, where possible, the roadbed. Although they were not faced with unmapped and mountainous terrain or the bone-chilling cold of the Alaska Highway, the Australian civilian and military engineers assigned to improve the Track had their own hazards to face.

The road south of Darwin had never been paved. This raw, dirt track would become choked with dust in the dry summer months and turn into a muddy quagmire during the wet season. Beginning in September 1940, construction crews started work on a 600-mile (965 km) section of road between Birdun, the terminus for the North Australian Railway, and Alice Springs in the Northern Territory. The work was completed by year's end, but the subsequent rainy season turned the three months of hard work into an impassable ribbon of mud that crossed creeks swollen with runoff. The Birdun–Alice Springs stretch would need to be rebuilt, this time as a paved, all-weather road with bridges across creeks and other waterways.

were hundreds of feet wide and subject to fast-moving spring-time floods fed by glacial melt from the mountains that would wash away anything less than the strongest structures.

The usual procedure was to first lay a pontoon bridge over the waterway. This allowed men and equipment to keep moving forward while temporary timber bridges were erected alongside them. Bridges were constructed out of timber that was downed to clear the roads and cut to the necessary lengths by the 35th

Priorities shifted when the U.S. military decided the Canadian oil pipeline was a more important project than the Alaska Highway. Government officials wanted to ensure a steady, reliable source of oil could be accessible within North America. Soldiers and engineers were transferred to the area to begin building roads (above) that would supply the pipeline project with materials.

Engineers' own sawmill, which itself was portable and could be moved up the road as the work progressed. Trucks delivered the freshly cut lumber to the work sites along with all of the necessary nuts and bolts and other hardware.

In some cases, bridges and sections of culvert were assembled at the sawmill and then brought to the site and put into place by a roving crane. Most of the structures, however, were too big for this procedure and had to be built piece by piece over the rivers and streams they bridged. Later, private construction company crews hired by the Public Roads Administration would follow. These crews replaced timber bridges with permanent steel structures, and they finished and paved the rough dirt and corduroy roads the military workers slashed through the wilderness.

The month of June saw increased activity, as the ground was finally dry enough that mud and silt were no longer a problem. The mood all along the highway was optimistic until July 9 or 10 when, without warning, the area was hit with the heaviest rains anyone could remember in more than 50 years. Heaviest hit were the several hundred miles around Fort Nelson. In those two days, the work of several weeks was undone: 24 of 25 bridges, countless culverts, and thousands of cubic yards of soil and gravel were washed away by the torrential downpour. The Muskwa River, where a 970-foot-long (296 m) bridge was under construction, rose 34 feet (10 m) overnight, washing away a construction crane and 300 barrels of fuel.

A month later, another downpour destroyed four bridges and brought mudslides that blocked several sections of completed road. The engineers had learned the costly lessons of the first rainstorm, however, and were prepared this time. The road was cleared and reopened within days.

Other bridges, such as the 300-foot (91 m) Sikanni Chief River Bridge, which was reconstructed in 1943, would be completely bypassed when the permanent roadbed was later laid by crews from the PRA. The original temporary bridge across the river was put up by one of the African-American regiments in less than

BRIDGING THE PEACE RIVER

The Peace River was a major waterway that had long been the main route for the lucrative northern Canadian fur trade. Though serviced by ferries, these were inadequate for the endless stream of supplies and equipment. As a result, a wooden trestle bridge—a type of bridge made up of many smaller spans supported on a longer frame—was first constructed in October 1942 at Taylor near Fort St. John. It was destroyed by the river's rushing waters within a month, and construction of a permanent steel suspension bridge was begun in December.

This permanent span was built by Roebling and Sons, the same company that had built the landmark Brooklyn Bridge across New York's East River, connecting Manhattan and Brooklyn more than 60 years earlier. Beginning in the last days of the winter of 1943, the piers and towers for the 2,130-foot-long (650 m) bridge were first erected directly on top of the frozen river. Over the course of just nine days, some 700 tons of steel roadways and supporting structure were set between them.

As the ice began to melt and break up, the towers and their great loads of steel were slipped off the ice and allowed to settle to the river bottom. According to a PRA report, "Then began the job of placing and adjusting the cable and erecting steelwork for the roadway." Steelwork and concrete roadway were completed on July 31, and the bridge was opened to traffic early in August. An erection job that, in a milder climate, would normally have taken eight months was accomplished in four months and one week.

The Peace River did not live up to its name as far as the bridge was concerned. The powerful current beat mercilessly against its piers. To strengthen and protect them from the pounding waters, engineers twice dumped tons of concrete and rock around them, in 1949 and 1952. These efforts were only a temporary fix; on October 16, 1957, the water had weakened the west pier enough to cause a section of it to collapse. The Canadians erected a new bridge, which was opened to traffic in January 1960 and still stands today.

four days and would last longer than any other bridge built during the original phase of construction. "We can't afford to lose our own personal pride by slipping up," said one of the troops involved in the construction on "Building the Alaska Highway."

For the most part, workers relied on temporary pontoon bridges, which could be floated into place quickly, and on log bridges built on the spot by workers who used handheld crosscut saws and local lumber felled by the crews as they cleared the path for the road. The priority was to have structures that spanned the water, no matter how temporary, so that construction could keep moving forward.

Northwest of Kluane Lake was the Donjek River, which would prove to be the most difficult river the crews spanned. The river, fed by glacial melt from the mountains, was wide and dangerous—especially during the springtime, when the ice broke up and created treacherous ice jams that could pound bridge supports to pieces. Crews tried to erect several log bridges across the Donjek, none of which survived for very long. Forty miles north, the White River, another glacial river, proved equally daunting until sturdier and more permanent bridges could be erected.

The longest trestle bridge along the route was the Nisutlin Bay Bridge at Teslin Lake at Johnson's Crossing. Because of the wartime shortage of steel, it would not be completed until 1944. At 2,300 feet (701 m) in length, the pilings, or foundations, for the approximately one-half-mile span had to be built on a thin layer of sand on top of a river bed that was mostly solid ice.

Today, only a single original timber bridge built in 1942 remains, over Canyon Creek in the Yukon Territory. Like other stretches of the original pioneer road, this short span is no longer part of the Alaska Highway. The route shifted in later years to accommodate permanent construction.

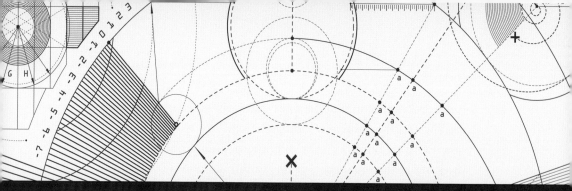

CHAPTER 5

"Nobody Else Knew the Mosquitoes Were There"

The construction of the Alaska Highway changed not only the map of the remote territories through which it ran but the entire social and economic profile of these areas as well. Before the territory opened up to settlers and tourists attracted by the highway, the construction crews of the military and the trailing PRA workers had to first survive some of the harshest conditions on Earth to complete this vital artery.

These workers faced not just cold weather but inferior living conditions, insects, and often dangerous methods of construction, especially in the early days of the project. "The mosquitoes were all over," said General Hoge in his memoirs. Despite the cold weather, mosquitoes and gnats were so bad that, according to Hoge, the soldiers had to wear protective netting at all times, even to eat their meals. "You would raise the head net and by the time you got food on the spoon up to your mouth it would be covered with mosquitoes. You were eating mosquitoes half the time, and then you had to pull (the net) right down again."

Alaska is home to 35 different species of mosquito, and the workers on the Alaska Highway did their best to stay away from all of them. Donning large-brimmed hats with netting to protect their heads and necks, the soldiers wore long shirts and pants (above) at all times in an attempt to cover every inch of skin from the blood-sucking insects.

Fortunately, unlike mosquitoes found in tropical climates, these were not dangerous. They were merely annoying: "They didn't carry malaria or anything else, but there were all kinds. They came right out of the snow. As the snow melted, you'd see them all over. Those were the big ones. They didn't sting so much and weren't so bad. As the ones (later in the season) got smaller, they were more vicious. I'd put my hand on my neck and pull it back and it would be covered with blood (from the mosquito bites)." It was not uncommon for workers to be incapacitated from swelling caused from bites.

"There was just droves of them," recalled Fred Mims, a lieutenant in the Quartermaster Corps attached to the highway project, on "Building the Alaska Highway." "(They would) come in clouds. We were issued those campaign hats with the (wide) brims, and pulled the nets down over and fastened them around

BUILDING AMERICA NOW

STUART HIGHWAY: AN ALL-WEATHER HIGHWAY

As soon as conditions allowed it in 1941, construction began anew on the highway between Alice Springs and Darwin, Australia. Although much of the 1,000 miles (1,609 km) laid through the Northern Territory would remain a dirt road, the engineers had learned that great stretches would need to be sealed, or paved, if they were to remain passable year-round.

Men, equipment, and supplies were transported to Alice Springs by rail. Included in the supplies was bitumen, the substance used to seal the roadbed and prevent it from turning to dust in the heat of summer and to mud in the wet season.

Australians often use the term *bitumen* to refer to any road surface. Bitumen is a naturally occurring sticky, tar-like substance that is refined from crude oil and is similar to tar. It is often used to pave streets and roads in America. Bitumen contains sulfur as well as heavy metals (for example, nickel, lead, and mercury) and toxic elements such as arsenic and selenium.

The Outback is a vast stretch of desolate landscape that lacks water and woodlands. Unlike the U.S. military engineers who constructed the Alaska Highway, the crews who laid down the Australian highway could not count on timber and other raw materials to be available along the route. Other than dirt from nearby hills, which could be moved to fill in your neck. If you didn't have a mosquito net on, you'd get bites all over you."

Civilian engineer Wallace Lytle said, "You couldn't fight them off. There's no way, the mosquitoes just eat you up. You'd of just been welts all over your body. You couldn't take a shirt off. You

depressions along the route, the Australian crews had to truck in everything else. In fact, fresh supplies were almost impossible to come by; to adequately feed the highway crews and keep the Northern Territory supplied with fresh produce to supplement canned rations, the army set up farms along the route.

Fuel dumps were also established all along the route. The trucks that moved continuously along the Track—and along the connecting road to staging areas in the west coast city of Adelaide—consumed vast quantities of gasoline due to strong head winds and the heavy loads they carried. In addition, there was a high rate of fuel evaporation in the storage drums exposed to the blistering sun and high temperatures of the region.

From 1941 to the end of the war in 1945, near continuous military convoys carrying men, equipment, supplies, and food moved up and down the newly developed highway between the northern and southern coasts of Australia. Trucks that carried almost 200,000 troops and all that accompanied them, as well as supplies and food for the civilian population in the Northern Territory, drove an estimated 100 million miles (160 million km) along the Track. It was a lifeline that enabled Australia to endure and do its part to fight the war in the Pacific.

When the fighting was over, this well-established Track through the wilderness remained. Yet, more than three decades would pass before construction of a paved road the entire width of the continent was undertaken.

couldn't even roll your sleeves up. If the palms of gloves were wore out, you still wore them because keep the back of your hands from being bitten."

Hayward Oubre, another engineer, likened the insects to America's foes in the World War, saying, "You had mosquitoes that dive-bombed you. They'd dive like the Japanese with the dive-bombing. They'd dive and hit you." A *Time* magazine article from August 31, 1942, also compared the mosquitoes to aircraft, printing a joke popular among the workers on the highway: "Why, over at Watson Lake, a mosquito landed on the airport and they put 85 gallons of gas into it before they realized it wasn't a bomber."

WORK UNTIL YOU DROP

Yet, as with all other obstacles faced along this road, the soldiers could do nothing but keep working, 24 hours a day, 7 days a week: "We were working, I think, eight-hour shifts. Three eight-hour shifts," said General Hoge of the official schedule that had been set down for his crews. The reality in the field was often, however, quite different—and exhausting. Henry Geyer was a truck driver with the army engineers; he recalled this hard duty on "Building the Alaska Highway," saying simply, "You worked until you dropped." He added, "You had to do the job. You didn't like it. So you figured that you might as well enjoy it, because otherwise you'd have gone nuts."

Bob Batey, another engineer interviewed in the documentary, agreed. "In the summer, the sun was up all the time," he said, which resulted in impossibly long hours of sunlight at their northern location. "We were on 12-hour shifts. Half of the company was in the morning, and half at night. We worked all the time, seven days a week." "It was slave labor, is what it was," said Wallace Lytle. "We weren't prisoners, but wanting to get the job done, we'd done most anything to do it."

Whether their labors ended in the evening or the morning, the exhausted soldiers would lay their heads pretty much wherever they fell. "We was working so hard that by the time you got through at night, you rolled your sleeping bag out underneath a tree or in the bushes, and you crawled in it and sacked out," said Chester Russell, a former rodeo worker from California.

Alden Hacker was another engineer who vividly recalled the exhaustion that daily overcame these workers. "Seldom did we ever put a tent up and tie all of the corners together. Usually you put them up and just enough to hold them together, because they're only going to be there for the night. The next day, the cooks would have to tear them down, load them up, and move them up the road as close to the front as they could move."

"We worked twelve and fourteen hours a day in the rain and the flies and the mosquitoes made life miserable for us, particularly in the open mess camps," remembered Master Sergeant George H. Burke of the 95th Engineers in *The Alaska Highway*. "We had hardly any free time, and most of what we did have we spent playing cards or pitching horseshoes."

Everyone suffered from the combination of cold and lack of sleep. Mistakes were common and accidents were frequent. Damaged vehicles and machines could be towed to the nearest camp for repairs, but there were not enough tow trucks and spare parts to keep up with the demand. Wrecks were left to accumulate on the side of the road and, against army regulations, some wrecks would be stripped of spare parts to be used in the repair of other vehicles. According to one witness, "Each temporary base camp began to resemble a military junkyard."

Soldiers went for long stretches with no other company than that of their comrades. Although they were often overcome with exhaustion after the long day's labors, they keenly felt the isolation. On "Building the Alaska Highway," army engineer Chester Russell said, "There was nobody. There was absolutely nobody. As far as young sweetie pies up there . . . we never seen a lady." Fellow engineer William Griggs agreed, recalling, "We were completely isolated in most cases. At the beginning we were near some Indian villages, but most of the time we were completely isolated." Despite the hardships, isolation, and loneliness, the soldiers understood all too well the importance of the task they had been assigned.

Occasionally, movies would make their way to some of the camps, where men like Master Sergeant Burke—who had been a Washington, D.C., film projectionist before he was drafted—would show them on a 16-millimeter projector. Even rarer were visits by the United Service Organizations (USO), a charitable, nonprofit organization that provides entertainment and recreation to U.S. military stationed around the world. One such show featured violin virtuoso Yehudi Menuhin in concert in Whitehorse.

Such diversions were few and far between for the men of the Alaska Highway. An article in a 1942 issue of *Engineering News Record* put the situation in perspective: "There was no recreational program provided for soldiers or civilians, probably none could have been provided. Work, work, work, and more work was the only program—day and night, seven days a week."

An article in the *New York Times* from December 31, 1942, said,

> The boys who built the Alcan highway . . . (are mostly) drafted youth from the corners of America. . . . They do not like to be told now that they are heroic, for their job held no glamour for them. They met it with curses and sweat. But with only their endless work, and their beefs, their checkers and their profanity for amusement they have pounded a road from the outpost of the outside world at Dawson Creek straight through to the heart of Alaska. They have done it despite hell, high water, and above all, loneliness. Many of them are eager to get out of Alcan country and into actual battle. But perhaps no action can be more dramatic or demanding than that which they have faced.

Keeping everyone fed was another problem that faced the workers scattered along the length of the Alaska Highway. Engineers and workers would often not see fresh food for months at a time. They relied instead on C rations, or prepackaged meals that offered few options—usually vegetable hash, meat hash, or chili con carne. The limited menu soon had the soldiers resorting to the age-old practice of bartering with the locals for some relief from their steady diet of prepared canned meals. "We got so sick and tired of the chili con carne, we would send truckloads of chili con carne down to the Indian village and trade it off for fish" recalled engineer William Griggs. "And they said, 'We'll trade, but no more chili con carne.' They got tired of it, themselves."

"We lived on Spam and Vienna sausage," said Fred Mims, while Chester Russell recalled, "Pancakes . . . was the number

The lack of variety in foodstuffs created another hardship for the workers to endure while working on the Alaska Highway. Pancakes, canned meats, and frozen potatoes often were the only edible supplies on hand, though most soldiers were able to supplement their diet with local fish and game. *Above,* hungry soldiers take a break to refill their bellies around the fire.

one on the list. Pancakes. We ate pancakes three times a day there for about a month."

The *New York Times* article of December 31 described the conditions found in a typical camp:

> Potatoes are iron-hard and have to be thawed for many hours before they can be cooked. Pancake batter may be freezing on top, and burning where it touches the stove. Returned laundry arrives in a solid chunk, which has to be set beside the oil drum

AFRICAN-AMERICAN SOLDIERS

African-American soldiers were thought to be especially vulnerable to the cold and harsh conditions found in the north. Shockingly, the official U.S. Army position (as put forth by a study conducted by the Army War College, a training school for military officers) was "The Negro is careless, shiftless, irresponsible and secretive. . . . He is best handled with praise and by ridicule."

Indeed, the military was reluctant to even send African-American troops to work on the highway, for fear that they would not be able to keep up with their white counterparts on this vital and fast-moving project. It was, in fact, unofficial army policy to *not* send African-American troops places like Alaska and Canada because of the mistaken assumption that they were not capable of performing well in the extreme cold. Yet, a wartime shortage of troops following the Japanese attack on Pearl Harbor, before draftees and enlistees could be trained and shipped out, forced the use of black troops on this vital northern mission.

Although African-American soldiers made up about one-third of the troops assigned to the highway, they often were assigned the harshest jobs in the worst conditions, including doing the labor on the brutal CANOL pipeline project. They were used only because the better-trained and better-equipped white soldiers were needed for jobs deemed more important. The black workers were routinely underequipped, and little stove for days before a sock or a handkerchief can be pried loose. . . . At all times the cold is the omnipresent factor, it is cruel to both men and machines.

Time Magazine reported that "Out in the bush the only recreation is hunting and fishing . . . (soldiers) hunt to vary meals of corned beef, potatoes, lemonade, carrots, preserves and dried eggs, by adding moose and bear steaks, lake trout, spruce partridge (Yukon chickens), ptarmigan (a species of game bird),

thought was given to their physical well-being or safety. It was not unusual for supplies and equipment to go to white soldiers, leaving the African Americans to make do with hand tools. They labored for weeks at a time in brutal temperatures that could reach –60°F (–51°C), living on frozen rations and in drafty canvas tents.

"Blacks in uniform had to endure the Army's discriminatory racial policies," said historian Heath Twichell. "The frequent expressions of hostility and contempt they encountered from individual whites only made that experience all the more painful." African Americans who worked under white officers trained in these prejudicial beliefs faced difficult conditions. According to Twichell, "In the minds of most senior white officers, black troops were not as capable in terms of their technical efficiency and ability to use the equipment. There was an expectation that they would do poorly." Their every action became an effort to prove to the white officers and soldiers that they were as capable as anyone else.

Of course, as was ultimately proven by their records for most highway mileage built, the army vastly underestimated the intelligence and skill of their black soldiers. The durability of the 300-foot (91 m) Sikanni Chief River Bridge, which was constructed by African-American regiments in less than four days, was proof of this.

grouse, venison. At Swan Lake, for lack of regular (fishing) tackle a Signal Corps man made a line from telephone wire, hammered a fishing spoon out of a tin can and brought in strings of fat trout over the side of an assault boat."

WEATHERING THE WEATHER

The most difficult challenge faced by almost everyone involved in the highway project was the weather, especially in the late winter and early spring months at the beginning of the construction. Men shipped from the lower 48 states, even those from the most northerly locations, were stunned by the cold.

The men of the 35th Engineers had originally been trained for duty in the tropical conditions of the Pacific. As difficult as the heat and humidity of the tropics could be, it seemed like paradise compared to the unrelenting misery of the Arctic cold. The cabs of the large bulldozers and road graders that did the bulk of the work along the highway, clearing the way and smoothing the roadbed, were open to the elements. Even trucks offered only canvas tops and window curtains as protection from the subzero temperatures.

Most Americans had never encountered such harsh conditions, including temperatures that routinely hit –50° or –60°F (–45.5° to –51°C). For those who had come from the South, California, or even the more moderate temperatures of the Midwest, the change was brutal. The men had to be careful: Skin exposed to the air froze in minutes. It took only seconds for bare flesh to freeze to any metal surface it touched. There was always the danger of near-instant death for anyone who fell into freezing streams or rivers. "It was so cold," one private from New York was reported as saying, "that every time we had hot stew for chow, the stuff froze before we could eat."

Quartermaster Fred Mims, who had been a bus driver in South Carolina before enlisting in the army, used the cold-weather clothing and equipment designated by the army for

In the subzero temperatures of Yukon Territory, frozen equipment stalled progress as trains and trucks needed to be warmed up manually or dug out of the snow. Frostbite was also an enormous problem, as even the smallest patches of exposed skin could freeze and require medical attention. *Above*, men use a rotary plow to dig out the Yukon Route train filled with supplies from Skagway.

the extreme northern climate. These included sheepskin-lined trench coats, reversible parkas, fur helmets, lambskin caps, wool pants, goggles, and down sleeping bags. Yet, the woolen gloves and rubber boots were not enough to ward off the harsh conditions. Cases of frostbite, or the freezing of flesh from the extreme cold, were routine. Officers reported coming across heavy machine operators parked by the side of the road, in tears because of the cold.

The men were not the only ones to suffer from the intense cold. Machines were also affected. At temperatures as low as those faced by the army engineers, metal becomes brittle and breaks easily; a bulldozer's plow hitting a buried boulder could easily shatter. Truck and car axles that bumped over the deeply rutted frozen ground would snap. Engineer William Griggs said, "Trucks, we had to keep running 24 hours a day. If you didn't, you'd have to get underneath a truck with a blowtorch and heat up the transmission and the rear axle before it would move."

When the temperature dropped well below freezing, wrote Heath Twichell in *Northwest Epic,*

> the only way to restart a stalled vehicle was to build a fire under its oil pan, a procedure empathically not recommended by the Army's drivers' manuals. Fire posed other risks as well. Cold, exhausted men became drowsy and disoriented when exposed to sudden warmth. Although drivers stopping for a bit to eat after many hours behind the wheel did no real damage to themselves when they literally fell asleep in their plates, several soldiers found themselves with scorched clothing and minor burns after having toppled dizzily into a campfire while warming their hands.

Others reported that even antifreeze did not prevent a truck's radiator fluid from freezing. To prevent the frozen fluid from expanding and cracking the engine blocks, it would be drained and kept warm over a fire until it was time to restart the vehicle.

Engineers and workers alike were diligent in keeping their equipment in working order. "It was," said Griggs, "actually a fight for survival." Billy Connor put it bluntly: "Minor mistakes can be deadly. If your vehicle breaks down in the Arctic, walking a few miles can actually cost you your life."

Sanitation and personal hygiene were also problems for the men in the field. During the coldest winter months, the *New York*

Times reported, "Men bathe one limb at a time, making the complete cycle perhaps once in six to eight weeks." Toilet facilities were completely lacking, and, even in the warmer weather, the men were forced to improvise for something so simple as a bath. When summer temperatures hit 90° (32°C) and warmer, and job sites became choked with dust, the men would bathe in still near-freezing streams fed by glacial melt-off from the mountains. Others would fashion bathtubs out of 50-gallon drums and heat water over fire for the rare luxury of a hot bath.

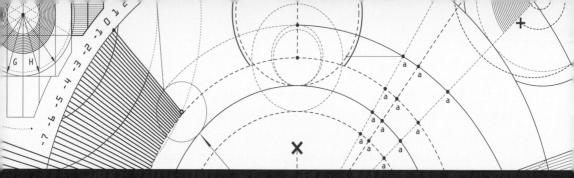

CHAPTER 6

"I Think Our Average Daily Mileage Was 14 Miles a Day"

Spring and summer brought renewed hope to the men build-ing the Alaska Highway. Unfortunately, it also brought new challenges, including the onset of mosquitoes, gnats, and black flies as well as the challenge of the melting permafrost exposed to the above-freezing temperatures. The northern section of the highway came to a virtual standstill, with as little as a single mile a day of road being completed until engineers came up with a solution to the sodden problem.

OTHER ROADS

Although the highway wound through territories largely un-known and unmapped by the army surveyors and engineers, this was not entirely unexplored territory. The area's indigenous peoples and settlers had long traveled and traded along the general region that was selected as the highway's corridor. In addition, as has been noted, it passed through—and, in many instances, destroyed—numerous settlements and villages. So quick was the progress of the highway that Canadian and

Alaskan natives received no advance notice of the changes headed their way. These communities did not learn about the highway until they heard the approaching bulldozers tearing through the forests.

The fact that these routes had long been in use pointed the surveying teams to them, often with the aid of the natives hired by the military to guide them through the wilderness. Their guides took advantage of many miles of traditional trails, which offered proven paths through virgin forests and mountainous terrain.

Crews worked south to north from Fort Nelson to Whitehorse—the project's major staging area as the railhead for the White Pass and Yukon Railway—and from Whitehorse toward the end of the road at Fairbanks. Others were hard at work chopping their way north from Valdez, Alaska, laying the road to the Yukon border to the southeast on the Gulf of Alaska.

Like the Richardson and Glenn highways, the Haines Cutoff Road was not an official part of the Alaska Highway, although its construction was considered vital to the larger project. Authorized in November 1942, the 160-mile (257 km) road was designed to connect the port of Haines, Alaska—located approximately 400 miles (644 km) south of Valdez on the Gulf of Alaska—with the Alaska Highway. The Haines Cutoff served several purposes: It provided an alternate route to the Alcan in the event that the White Pass and Yukon Railway was blocked by weather, attack, or accident; it serviced a second seaport for the delivery and shipment of supplies; and it offered a means of mass evacuation for the population, if necessary. The Cutoff Road, which passed through parts of Alaska, British Columbia, and the Yukon Territory, took 13 months and more than $13 million to build.

Other, smaller roads and trails could be found along the length of the highway. At the southern starting point of the highway in Canada's British Columbia, Dawson Creek and Fort St. John were connected by a 48-mile (77 km) route. Farther north, the route between Whitehorse and Kluane Lake in the

Yukon Territory—which linked mining camps at Silver City and a trading center at Burwash Landing—was serviced by 150 miles (241 km) of wagon road.

Although the majority of workers along the highway were with the military, there were not enough troops available for

THE RICHARDSON HIGHWAY

Crews did not need to cut every mile of the highway from scratch, but the existing roads were neither extensive nor, for the most part, any more developed than the Alaska Highway itself. Fairbanks, Alaska, already had a fairly substantial—if quite rough—road in the Richardson Highway, the first major highway to have been built in the territory.

Like the White Pass and Yukon Railway, the Richardson Highway had been constructed during the Klondike gold rush, following the 1896 discovery of gold in the Yukon. Like the Alaska Highway then under construction, it too had been a project of the U.S. military, providing an American-operated route to the gold fields in the Klondike. The original 409-mile (660 km) road, hardly more than a pack trail for prospectors, miners, and their mules and small wagons, was constructed from the port at Valdez to Eagle. The army kept the trail open after the gold rush subsided to serve as a connection between Fort Liscum in Valdez and Fort Egbert in Eagle.

A second gold rush in 1902 prompted the construction of a telegraph line along the trail, which increased its importance as an access road into the Alaskan interior. Eight years later, the Alaska Road Commission upgraded the rough road to a more usable wagon road. The upgrade was headed by General Wilds P. Richardson (in whose honor the highway would later be named), and the work was done by both regular construction workers and failed gold prospectors.

The road was again upgraded in the 1920s to handle the rise of automotive traffic that had by then reached the far north. Tolls on commercial vehicles, which could cost as much as $175 per trip, were later instituted to help pay for road maintenance and construction.

the job at hand. The Public Roads Administration hired private contractors, many of whom worked under the supervision of general contractors Lytle and Green, an Iowan company that had been hired to build facilities near Delta for the Northwest Staging Route. With the short construction season of 1942 drawing to a

Though not technically a part of the Alaska Highway, the Richardson Highway was a vital connection from the coast to the highway proper. Another preexisting stretch of road, the Glenn Highway—which was first laid out as the Palmer Road in the 1930s—connected Anchorage, Alaska, near the military base of Merrill Field northwest of Valdez to the agricultural colony of Glenn, 187 miles (301 km) to the northeast. During the course of the construction of the Alaska Highway, the Palmer Road was extended to reach Glennallen on the Richardson Highway. The Tok Cutoff, a section of the Glenn Highway (named for Captain Edwin Glenn, who led the 1898 army expedition that blazed the Alaska route to the Klondike), extended the highway's length to 328 miles (528 km). Crews working for the Public Roads Administration were put to work improving the Richardson Highway into Fairbanks.

The Richardson Highway was by no means an easy piece of work for the construction crews, who were brought in by ship at Valdez in April. The road needed to be cleared of the deep winter snows and widened to render it passable, especially over a treacherous portion of the route through Thompson Pass. This job was assigned to the 97th Engineers, one of the African-American regiments. The workers, however, were not given the proper training or adequate equipment to do the necessary work of quickly opening this stretch of road to truck convoys needed to ferry men and supplies from the port at Valdez to the main construction corridor. It took two months for 78 miles (125 km) of road to be hacked out of the wagon road.

The stretch of the Alaska Highway that took the longest to construct was the mile near Kluane Lake. The lake is surrounded by granite cliffs, quicksand, and permafrost, and it was one of the biggest challenges of the project. Using dynamite and jackhammers, workers had to cut through the rock to make room for the highway *(above)*.

close, they were given a contract to work on the highway itself and brought in several small road-building companies from their home and neighboring states.

TOWNS AND OUTPOSTS ALONG THE WAY

An abandoned construction camp east of Tanacross was taken over by residents of that town and became a new village they called Dot Lake. An airstrip that had been built by the residents— by hand—in 1935 had by 1942 become a bustling center of activity and home to 1,000 soldiers who had enlarged and paved the strip. Later, the village would move across the river for better access to the road, taking over another abandoned highway construction site. All along the route of the Alaska Highway, outposts, villages, and towns were reshaped, moved, or created in response to the great project.

The men of the 97th reached the Tok Cutoff in late August. From there, they transferred their efforts to the Alaska Highway itself. They began construction southeast in a race to meet the men of the 18th Engineers, the regiment that worked on the final stretch of the highway building east from Kluane. The intersection of the Richardson Highway and the Tok Cutoff became a base camp that would eventually grow into a town called Tok.

Another town created from what was originally a temporary camp for construction workers was Delta Junction. It grew out of the junction of the old Richardson and the new Alaska Highway at a location formerly known as Buffalo Junction, originally a construction camp used by the Depression-era Civilian Conservation Corp (a government agency created in 1933 to offer work on civic improvement programs to the unemployed).

One of the most profoundly affected towns was Dawson Creek, British Columbia, at "Mile 0," or the start of the highway. Dawson Creek, which had a population of about 600, was named after Canadian geologist George Dawson, who had first surveyed the area in 1879. The railroad reached the town in 1931, but the town did not experience the first signs of explosive growth until the arrival in early 1942 of the first troops assigned to build the Alaska Highway. Eventually, 20,000 people were jammed into this small town; they strained its every resource and filled every

BUILDING AMERICA NOW

STUART HIGHWAY: A MODERN HIGHWAY AT LAST!

Today, traveling the Stuart Highway is considered one of the easiest journeys of any major Australian highway. Yet, the upgrade from crudely sealed bitumen highway and long stretches of dirt road did not begin until 1978. Nearly 20 years would pass before the highway was officially completed and opened to traffic from one end of the country to the other.

Surveys of the route had to be taken before construction began, a process that took five years to complete. Because of the harsh climate and heat along much of the route through the Outback, work could only be done in the cooler months between April and October. Grading, filling, and, in some cases, changing the route were undertaken, often on the advice of Aboriginal—as the indigenous Australian people are known—advisers. These advisers were consulted for the first time in the road's more than century-long history about where and how the road should cross their lands.

The well-being of construction crews was also of concern to the Department for Transport, Energy, and Infrastructure, the Australian government agency in charge of roads and their maintenance. Small towns sprang up along the length of the highway project, which allowed crews and their families to remain together during the long project.

Until 1980, much of the 1,689-mile (2,719 km) length of the Stuart Highway was dirt surface, often subject to closure for long periods due to rains that turned them to mud or caused flash flooding. More modern available warehouse, barn, and stable with supplies and equipment for the men and the road they were building north toward Fairbanks.

techniques, including the construction of more stable roadbeds and drainage systems, were put into effect along the entire stretch of the road. Much of the World War II–era bitumen surface was removed and replaced. When the Stuart Highway was officially opened on March 24, 1987, by Federal Minister for Transport Peter Morris, little if any of the original sealed surface survived.

Construction continues all along the Stuart Highway. A mining boom in parts of South Australia has led to the need for better and wider highways to accommodate the increase in traffic and trucking. Paved surfaces have also deteriorated over the years under the harsh heat of the Outback. The effort and cost of maintaining the highway led the government to institute a program of upgrades to the Track. Among other issues, the upgrade program—which will continue into 2009—will widen lanes to a uniform 11.5 feet (3.5 m), with 3.2-foot-wide (1 m) shoulders, large enough to accommodate the giant dump trucks, tandem trailers, and other vehicles that will need to use the road in the coming years. Additional and upgraded service areas will also be added along the route, where towns and outposts can be hundreds of miles apart.

Today's Stuart Highway has evolved into far more than the original dirt Track through the Outback. The modern Stuart is no longer just a highway but a high-tech corridor through which run not only the historic Track but a transcontinental railroad, gas and water pipelines, power and fiber-optic communications lines, and microwave towers. Far from being a line between the south and north coasts, it has grown into a vital lifeline that links all points of Australia.

Even after the disastrous fire and explosion that killed five people in February 1943, progress on the highway did not slow. The town rebuilt and, even after the road was complete and the army and private contractors were gone, Dawson Creek remained prosperous thanks to the flood of travelers, tourists, and truckers that steadily rumbled through. In the 1950s, natural gas was discovered at Fort St. John; by 1986, the area would boast a population of 50,000, many of whom were employed by the gas-processing plants and refineries nearby.

THE NORTHWEST STAGING ROUTE

Watson Lake, a town in the Yukon Territory, was another stop along the Northwest Staging Route, as well as one of the major bases for the construction of the highway. So was Northway, Alaska, where a major air base was established.

Fort St. John—located on the banks of the Peace River, about 50 miles (80 km) north of Dawson Creek—began as a fur trading post in 1806 but did not become a town of any consequence until 1941, when it became home to one of the air bases along the Northwest Staging Route. Fort Nelson, the next link on the highway about 350 miles (563 km) to the north, was another early trading post where the establishment of a stop along the Northwest Staging Route caused a sudden growth spurt.

Whitehorse, on the banks of the Yukon River, was the largest town along the Canadian section of the route. It was founded during the Klondike gold rush of 1896, where it served as the northern end of the White Pass and Yukon Railway, running between Whitehorse and Skagway, Alaska, a distance of 110 miles (117 km). In addition to serving as a supply point for the boats that traveled the Yukon River, an airport had been constructed there in 1929. The Northwest Service Command, in charge of the Northwest Staging Route—as well as all supply and construction operations of the U.S. Army in northern Canada—was set up in Whitehorse in September 1942.

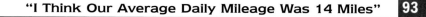
The last stop on the highway was Fairbanks, Alaska, one of interior Alaska's major cities. Fairbanks had its beginning in the gold rush of the early 1900s and was linked to Anchorage, Alaska, and the sea by the Alaska Railroad. Although the original urgency to build the Alaska Highway and set up the Northwest Staging Route was a defensive one, to protect against a Japanese invasion of North America, the actual military strategy in the northern Atlantic soon changed that. In May 1943, 12,000 American troops would invade the Aleutian Island of Attu, but they were transported there by ships from the American West Coast rather than along the highway.

The highway and the staging route airfields it serviced would find their usefulness in the Lend-Lease Program with Russia. Fairbanks proved to be the hub of the Alaskan/Siberian ferry route by which the Russian military was kept supplied with desperately needed U.S.-manufactured fighter planes and bombers to fight Nazi Germany in Eastern Europe. The aircraft were brought to Fairbanks's Ladd Field along the Northwest Staging Route and then flown by Russian pilots over the Bering Strait, which separates the westernmost point of North America from the easternmost point of the Asian continent by 58 miles (92 km). Then they flew across Siberia—a vast, frozen section of northern Asia—to Moscow and Leningrad, where Russia defended against overwhelmingly powerful Nazi forces. Almost 8,000 aircraft were delivered to the Russians at Ladd Field. The first flight of 10 A-20 attack bombers took off on September 29, 1942.

The Northwest Staging Route airfields all had at least one runway in operation by the end of 1942. Yet, as the amount of air traffic that passed along this vital supply route increased, so did the need for improvements. Not until late 1943 were the bases at Fort Nelson, Watson Lake, and Northway equipped with all-weather navigation aids, adequate maintenance facilities, and additional runways to handle the increased air traffic. Some of this slow progress was due to conditions along the Alaska

Highway itself. During the winter of 1942–1943, stretches of the highway remained closed because of poor weather conditions, flooding, or the upgrading and rebuilding of sections by the PRA.

Canadian labor unions and contracting companies objected to the work on the Canadian airfields being done by the American military and civilian contractors. They claimed that it robbed their countrymen of jobs. The Canadian government in Ottawa also did not like that the airfields were being built solely to answer the needs of American military air traffic. Eventually, the war would be over and the airfields would be turned over to Canadian control for use by its civilian aviation industry. The Canadian government felt it should have control over the final layout of the fields on its soil and that its workers should be building them.

Ultimately, an excess of Canadian bureaucratic red tape and problems with the unions forced Canada to cede control of most of the construction of the Northern Staging Route on its soil to the United States. Canada would, however, pay back the United States for most of the $120 million it cost to upgrade and maintain the fields during the war.

THE LAST MILES

As the summer of 1942 raced to an end, so did efforts to finish the rough pioneer road. By late September, the last miles between Watson Lake and Fort Nelson were being opened by the bulldozers of the 35th Engineers, who worked southeast from Watson Lake, and by those of the 340th, bearing northwest from Fort Nelson.

They met, at last, in the middle of a small tributary of the Laird River now known as Contact Creek. Bulldozers from both units crashed through the dense underbrush on either bank of the creek. At 5:00 P.M. on September 24, the bulldozers met nose to nose in midstream. Although these last miles of road in either direction from Contact Creek would need to be filled and graded

The first truck to run from Dawson Creek to Fairbanks is flanked by soldiers (*above*). After eight months of construction, the highway was put to use, although it was not entirely complete.

before they could truly be called a road, the meeting of the two units was symbolic, and the army used it to great public relations benefit. Knowing they were only days away from this moment, the army had—two days earlier—sent two soldiers, Corporal Otto Gronke and Private First Class Robert Bowe, on the first official trip along the "completed" highway in a half-ton weapons carrier.

Corporal Gronke and Private Bowe drove the 1,030 miles (1,658 km) between Dawson Creek and Whitehorse in 71 hours over 5 days at an average speed of 15 mph (24 kph). The going was slow, but they survived the journey over muddy roads, up steep grades, and around hairpin turns with the only incident of note being a single flat tire. They were photographed on September 27 shaking hands with a member of the Canadian North West Mounted Police, their truck freshly painted with a sign declaring it "First Truck, Dawson Creek to Whitehorse." Three days later, regularly scheduled supply runs began daily travel along the route.

The African-American soldiers of the 97th Engineers, who had been working on improving and extending the Richardson Highway, reached the flatlands of the Tok River basin near Big Delta late in August. From there, they turned their attention to the Alaska Highway itself. They cut the road southeast from the Tok Cutoff, where they would eventually meet up with the crews of the 18th Engineers working up from Kluane. This 100-mile (161 km) portion south of Fairbanks was the last stretch of road to be cleared; it cut across the border between Alaska and Canada near Northway.

Both regiments were making slow progress, which was especially frustrating to the men of the 18th. The 150 miles they had cut from Whitehorse to Kluane during June and early July had set a record for mileage made by any regiment, but the permafrost encountered on this final leg of the project was an obstacle that could not be dealt with by any other means than slow and careful work.

Rather than sending teams of bulldozers through to knock down trees and scrape away undergrowth, the vegetation had to be cut by hand and left where it fell as insulation against the sun's warming rays. Layers of logs and brush were laid on top of this, compressed by bulldozers, and followed by yet another layer of gravel and dirt—as many as 1,000 truckloads a day. In *Northwest Epic*, historian Heath Twichell described the results of this effort as "bulldozers then spread and shaped this top-

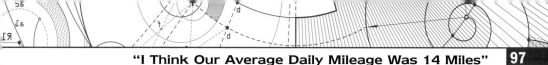

ping into an approximation of the final roadway and graders and rollers finished the job. Snaking cross-country from horizon to horizon, the result looked like an endless dike or berm, little more than 25 feet [7.6 m] wide at its base and 2 to 4 feet [0.7 to 1.2 m] high, with a narrow dirt road on top. Building a half mile [0.8 km] of such a road was a hard day's work for an entire Engineer regiment."

Kluane Lake, which measured 40 miles (64 km) long and as much as 6 miles (10 km) wide, was another challenge. It featured stretches of quicksand and a mile (1.8 km) of roadway that had to be blasted out of the granite cliffs lining its western shore. Beyond Kluane Lake, the permafrost kept the 18th Engineers down to an average of about 5 miles (8 km) of finished road a week for the 6 weeks it took to complete a 32-mile (51 km) stretch south of the Donjek River.

The 18th and the 97th met in the vicinity of Beaver Creek on October 25, 1942. Once again, the African-American troops—originally denigrated by white superior officers and fellow troops—proved they could handle the work just as well, if not better, than anyone else. In this last leg of their work on the highway, they beat their white counterparts in the 18th Engineers in the number of miles constructed. The news photograph of the meeting showed a black soldier, Corporal Refines Sims Jr. of Pennsylvania, and a white one, Private Alfred Jalufka from Texas, shaking hands from their bulldozers.

According to the Department of War at the time, 10,000 soldiers and 2,000 civilian workmen built the road in slightly more than 6 months. They averaged 8 miles (13 km) of the 24-foot-wide (7 m) roadway a day, building bridges over 200 streams, and some of the road reached an altitude of 4,212 feet (1,284 m).

Of course, as was the case at Contact Creek, there was still work to be done filling, grading, and leveling the roughly cut road left behind by both regiments. Yet, on October 29, Secretary of War Henry Stimson announced, "Trucks started to roll the entire

1,671 mile [2,689 km] length of the Alcan Highway this week." Although the official opening ceremonies would not be held until Sunday, November 15, on the border of Alaska and Canada, the Alaska Highway was—for the purposes of "carrying soldiers and supplies to Alaskan posts"—completed.

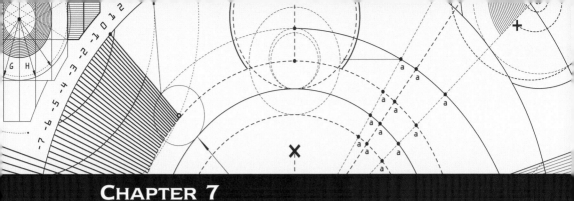

CHAPTER 7

"I'm Not Sure if the Road's Finished Today"

General Hoge was relieved of command of the Alaska Highway project in September 1942 and reassigned to Fort Knox, Kentucky, where he trained to command armored divisions of tanks. "We had gotten trucks through when I left," he recalled in his memoirs, published in 1993. "We didn't have the road finished. Actually, I'm not sure if the road's finished today."

The highway's official opening ceremony was held as scheduled, 162 miles (260.7 km) north of Whitehorse. Two hundred invited guests stayed at a newly constructed barracks building and feasted on a banquet of moose steak and roast mountain sheep. Brass bands played and speeches were made before the ribbon-cutting ceremony took place in the –15°F (–26°C) weather. Yet, for all the pomp and circumstance, the highway was still little more than a rough supply route. It would be a long time before it could truly be considered a proper highway.

The winter of 1942 was one of the coldest on record, with temperatures reaching –70°F (–56.6°C). Nonetheless, the army was under orders to keep the highway open as a supply line. In addition, the men were to begin construction on the Haines Cutoff, a road that linked the port city of Haines to the highway midway between Whitehorse and Kluane Lake. The Haines Cutoff would enable cargo brought in by sea and headed for the northern end of the highway to bypass the congested southern section of road.

In addition to the extreme cold, the engineers had to contend with 30-foot-deep (9 m) snowdrifts and an Arctic ice phenomenon that no one had ever encountered: rivers and streams that froze from the *bottom* up. The swiftly moving waters would prevent the surface from freezing while the thickening bottom

The U.S. military celebrated with an opening ceremony for the highway on Soldier's Summit beside Kluane Lake. Used as propaganda to boost wartime morale in the United States, the splashy event featured a brass band, speeches, and an elaborate banquet during one of the coldest months of the year. *Above*, the official ribbon-cutting ceremony.

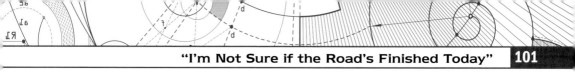

The dramatic differences between winter and summer posed unique problems for the construction and maintenance of the Alaska Highway. Bridges were submerged by rising waters in the winter, then washed away in the rushes of the summer thaw. *Above*, a truck is stuck in rising waters as an ice bridge collapses in Teslin.

ice pushed the icy waters higher and flooded the surrounding countryside. Bridges were literally swallowed by ice from below; come the spring thaw, they were swept away by the force of the receding waters. This problem was particularly acute along the northernmost stretches of the highway in Canada, from the Donjek River to Big Delta in Alaska.

MAINTENANCE AND IMPROVEMENTS

Activity in Dawson Creek continued as the need for supplies grew in response to the demands of road improvements and permanent facilities all along the route. Colonel Heath Twichell, commander of Dawson Creek, wrote to his wife in November 1942 of "the tremendous stores needed to put the road in operation. . . . the materials—nails, lumber, roofing paper and the like, and labor, fast enough to build warehouses for incoming goods. Usually a warehouse will be full before the roof is up." He wrote of having "shoved stuff North as fast or faster than it arrived." The first priority was "the material needed to house the troops, mostly steel huts . . . which are really quite warm and comfortable and can be erected quickly," but they faced "hundreds of new problems (that had to be) met and overcome in the operation of the road. . . . Providing shops for instance, for repairing all the thousands of trucks that will be in operation this winter, huge parts warehouses, protection against freezing for rations, and a host more."

Reliable communication along the highway was the latest priority. The $4.3 million Canadian Telephone project erected poles and strung telephone and teletype wires along the length of the highway, as well as to every military installation along its length and a branch line north to the Canadian oil fields. The civilian contractors hired to erect the 2,000 miles (3,219 km) of wires between Edmonton, Ontario, Canada, and Fairbanks, Alaska, were—like the military construction workers who came before them on the highway itself—unprepared for the harsh winter conditions. They found the ground frozen harder than steel; along one stretch of 442 miles (711 km) in the dead of the subarctic winter, they were forced to put aside the usual digging tools and use dynamite to blast holes in which to plant telephone poles.

The Public Road Administration was tasked with keeping the pioneer road plowed and passable during the winter months. Conflicting orders by military commanders had caused many workers to be sent home, however, which left much of the work to be done by the military.

In early 1943, the PRA began to upgrade the rough pioneer road that made up much of the Alaska Highway's mileage. Their

Built from an initial reaction of fear and vulnerability in wartime, the Alaska Highway was an epic undertaking by the U.S. military. Eleven regiments of men, many of whom had never experienced the Alaskan wilderness, completed one of the greatest engineering feats in the harshest of climates in a mere eight months. Though the road is no longer used strictly for military purposes, it is often frequented by tourists who are attracted to the spectacular Alaskan scenery.

job was to keep it in passable conditions on a year-round basis. They had to widen it where necessary to a width of 26 to 32 feet (8 to 10 m), straighten its hairpin turns, reduce grades to the maximum allowable 10 degrees, lay new roadbeds across vast stretches of swampy areas, and replace the hundreds of temporary wooden bridges with permanent steel structures.

Workers for private construction companies hired by the PRA, who had gained experience working in the harsh Arctic conditions during the initial construction season of 1942, began to replace the military engineer regiments. By mid-1943, more than 16,000 civilian construction workers were at work along the American and Canadian stretches of the highway. Fort St. John and Whitehorse served as the PRA's main headquarters to oversee this army of civilian workers.

The PRA's goal was to get the road in such shape that would allow year-round, all-weather access. Pavement and permanent bridge decking were not a priority; finishing the road by the army's October 1943 deadline was. On October 13 of that year, the Utah construction company finished work on the last and most problematic stretch of road, a muskeg- and permafrost-plagued section northwest of Kluane Lake.

By the end of the month, civilian workers were being sent home. Whatever work remained to be done on a few bridges was handed back to the military engineers. The army would have the responsibility of maintaining and repairing the road for the rest of the war, but it hired crews for the actual work from the ranks of the departing Canadian construction workers.

The last American to work on the Canadian section of the Alaska Highway was PRA maintenance consultant Frank C. Turner. He stayed on until April 1946, eight months after the war ended, when Canada formally assumed control of its own section of the highway.

THE ALCAN TODAY

In many ways, General Hoge's assertion that the Alaska Highway was not finished even more than 30 years after the project began remains true even today, another 30 or more years later. According to the *Out West* travel newspaper "Almost all of the two-lane highway is surfaced with asphalt," but "there still are stretches where the highway is narrow and curvy, where it lacks center lines and ample shoulders. Also, watch out for sudden loose-gravel breaks where the pavement has failed or is under repair. . . . And that asphalt paving can ripple like a roller coaster track in places where 'frost heaves' are caused by seasonal freezing and thawing of the ground."

Work on the highway has never really stopped, and today's road bears little resemblance to the World War II–era "muddy, twisting, single-lane trail fit only for trucks and bulldozers." Said Lynn Gabriel, deputy director of the Great Alaska Highways Society, "Some people still have the perception that they're going to be driving up through the wilderness and they need 17 spare tires and armor plates to punch their way through."

The highway as it was originally planned and constructed was 1,671 miles (2,689 km) long. Since October 1943, efforts taken to straighten the road and eliminate detours around obstacles have reduced the mileage between Dawson Creek and Fairbanks to 1,488 miles (2,395 km). The distance between Seattle, Washington, in the lower 48 states and Fairbanks, Alaska, is 2,313 miles (3,722 km). The Alaska Highway has become a tourist attraction for Americans and Canadians alike, many of whom drive the entire length of this historic route with no other destination beyond the trip itself. Tourists are advised to allow a week to 10 days for the drive.

More than 80 years since Canadian highway engineer Donald MacDonald began his crusade to create a highway through the great and unmapped wilderness of two nations, and nearly 70 years since the attack on Pearl Harbor, Hawaii, made the highway a vital component in the fight against America's enemies in the northern Pacific and Asia, the Alaska Highway has become part of the vast North American highway system. It links the United States not only with Canada but also with its own northern territories in Alaska. It has proven itself, in both capacities, a modern wonder of engineering.

CHRONOLOGY

1867 The United States purchases the 663,267 square miles of the Alaskan Territory from Russia for $7.2 million, or approximately .02¢ per acre.

1896 *August* Gold is discovered along the Klondike River near Dawson City in Alaska's Yukon Territory, bringing a stampede of an estimated 40,000 people to this remote northern area.

1898 Construction of the White Pass and Yukon Railway begins; the U.S. Congress authorizes funds for development of a telegraph line running from Seattle, Washington, to Sitka, Alaska, on the Gulf of Alaska.

TIMELINE

1867
The United States purchases the 663,267 square miles of the Alaska Territory from Russia for $7.2 million, or approximately .02¢ per acre.

1928
Donald MacDonald, an engineer with the Alaskan Road Commission, proposes the idea for a highway that would connect the lower 48 states with Alaska and the Yukon Territory via Canada.

1867 —— 1941

1941
December 7 The Japanese attack America's naval base at Pearl Harbor, Hawaii, signaling the beginning of U.S. involvement in World War II.

1904 North West Mounted Police officer Major Constantine is sent to open a trail to the gold fields of the Canadian Yukon, building 375 miles (603 km) of road between Fort St. John and the Stikine River before the project is cancelled. A telegraph line from Seattle, Washington, to Valdez, Alaska, begins operation.

1905 *January 27* Congress creates the Alaska Road Commission, which is authorized to build the territory's first proper roads.

1915 Construction begins on the Alaska Railroad to connect Seward to Fairbanks.

1923 *July 13* The 470-mile (756 km) Alaska Railroad between Seward and Fairbanks is completed at a cost of $65 million.

1942
February 7 The chief of staff of the U.S. Army approves the Alaska Highway project.

March 8 Construction of the Alaska Highway officially begins.

1942 ⋙ 1948

September 24 The northern and southern segments of the highway meet at Contact Creek, marking the completion of the Alaska Highway.

1948
The Alaska Highway is open to limited public access.

1928 Donald MacDonald, an engineer with the Alaskan Road Commission, proposes the idea for a highway that would connect the lower 48 states with Alaska and the Yukon Territory via Canada.

1933 Congress, in response to lobbying by the International Highway Association, a group headed by Donald MacDonald, authorizes President Roosevelt to initiate a joint U.S.-Canadian commission to study a road to Alaska.

1939 *May 14* Alaskan fur trapper Clyde "Slim" Williams and his partner John Logan begin a five-month journey by motorcycle from Fairbanks, Alaska, to the lower 48 states on a trip designed to promote the need for Donald MacDonald's proposed highway.

November 7 The joint U.S.-Canadian Alaskan International Highway Commission reports that the highway is a " 'worthy and feasible project' of reasonable cost."

1941 *December 7* The Japanese attack America's naval base at Pearl Harbor, Hawaii, signaling the beginning of U.S. involvement in World War II.

1942 *February 7* The chief of staff of the U.S. Army approves the Alaska Highway project.

February 11 President Roosevelt authorizes the immediate beginning of construction of the Alaska Highway.

February 14 Brigadier General William M. Hoge arrives in Alaska to inspect the proposed route and take command of the Alaska-Canada highway project.

March 2 The first crews, the men of the 35th Engineer Regiment (Combat), arrive in Dawson Creek, British Columbia, on the Northern Alberta Railroad from Edmonton.

March 8 Construction of the Alaska Highway officially begins.

May 15 A makeshift barge transporting men and equipment across Charlie Lake capsizes in a sudden storm, killing 12 soldiers.

May After two months of work, only 95 miles (152 km) of highway have been built.

June 3 The Japanese attack the American base at Dutch Harbor in the Aleutian Islands, 750 miles west of the Alaskan coastline, and seize two islands at the western end of the island chain.

June In improving weather, 295 miles (475 km) of road are finished during the month.

July Progress increases, with an additional 400 miles (644 km) of road finished.

September 24 The northern and southern segments of the highway meet at Contact Creek, marking the completion of the Alaska Highway.

November 20 The Alaska Highway is officially dedicated at Soldier's Summit with the arrival of the first truck convoy from Whitehorse to Fairbanks.

1946 *April 1* The U.S. Army officially transfers control of the Canadian portion of the Alaska Highway to the Canadian army, Northwest Highway System.

1948 The Alaska Highway is open to limited public access.

GLOSSARY

Arctic   The region near or at the North Pole that is character-
ized by low temperatures and hostile environments.

berm   A mound of earth formed to control the flow of surface
water.

corduroy road   A roadbed built up with logs laid tightly together;
named for the rough texture of the fabric.

culvert   A pipe used to direct water away from the surface and
under the road.

elevation   The height of a geographical location in relation to a
specific fixed point, usually sea level.

engineer   A person professionally trained in creative, scientific,
and technological specialties to plan and create mechanical
or physical structures for a variety of uses.

frostbite   The freezing of flesh exposed to extreme cold.

gauge   The distance between two rails; standard gauge in the
United States is 56.5 inches (143.5 cm).

grade   The angle, or gradient, of the slope of a road or other
surface.

Great Divide   The division in the North American continent
formed by the Rocky Mountains.

muskeg   A swamp or bog formed by thousands of years of
accumulated decayed vegetative matter; common to glacial
regions.

Northwest Staging Route   A series of airports, airstrips, and
radio directional stations placed every 100 miles (160 km)
from British Columbia across the Yukon to Alaska, connected by the Alaska Highway.

Panama Canal   The 40-mile-long (64 km) ship canal built by
the United States across the Isthmus of Panama between
1904 and 1914 to connect the Atlantic Ocean with the Pacific
Ocean, cutting 8,000 miles (12,875 km) from the journey by
ship between New York and San Francisco.

permafrost A layer of soil at varying depths below the surface that has remained continuously frozen for anywhere from a few to many thousands of years.

pioneer road The first rough road through a wilderness area, usually unpaved.

pontoon A flat-bottomed boat, or the floats used to support a structure on water.

prefabricated Standardized sections that are preassembled in a factory or other location to be shipped and assembled at a building site.

Public Roads Administration The U.S. government agency charged with overseeing and maintaining America's roads and highways.

Quartermaster Corps The unit of the military that specialized in supplying and provisioning troops.

siding A short stretch of railroad track used to store railcars or to allow trains on the same line to pass one another.

silt A rock or mineral particle smaller than very fine sand and larger than coarse clay.

surveyor One who determines the boundaries and elevations of the land through the three-dimensional measurement of points and the distances and angles between them.

trestle A timber, reinforced concrete, or steel structure— usually consisting of many short spans—used to support a temporary or permanent bridge or to temporarily construct a bridge.

United States Army Corps of Engineers A division of the U.S. Army whose mission is to provide military and public works and engineering services in support of military actions and the public good, including dams, canals, military installations, and environmental regulations.

BIBLIOGRAPHY

"Barracks with Bath." *Time*, August 31, 1942. Available online: http://www.time.com/time/magazine/article/0,9171,850012,00.html

Cohen, Stan. *The Trail of '42: A Pictorial History of the Alaska Highway.* Missoula, Mont.: Pictorial Histories Publishing Company, 1979.

Griggs, William E. *The World War II Black Regiment That Built the Alaska Military Highway: A Photographic History.* Jackson, Miss.: University Press of Mississippi, 2002.

Haigh, Jane. *The Alaska Highway.* Whitehorse, Canada: Wolf Creek Books, 2000.

Public Broadcasting Service. "Building the Alaska Highway." *American Experience.* PBS.org. Available online: http://www.pbs.org/wgbh/amex/alaska/.

Twichell, Heath. *Northwest Epic: The Building of the Alaska Highway.* New York: St. Martins Press, 1992.

U.S. Army Corps of Engineers. "Engineer Memoirs: General William M. Hoge, U.S. Army." January 1993. Available online: http://www.usace.army.mil/publications/eng-pamphlets/ep870–1-25/toc.htm.

Alaska Highway Construction During World War II. DVD. College Park, Md.: National Archives of the United States, 2008.

American Experience: Building the Alaska Highway. DVD. Directed by Matthew Collins and Rocky Collins. PBS, 2005.

Bauer, Erwin, and Peggy Bauer. *The Alaska Highway: A Portrait of the Ultimate Road Trip*. Seattle, Wash.: Sasquatch Books, 2003.

Brown, Tricia. *The World-Famous Alaska Highway*. Portland, Ore.: Alaska Northwest Books, 2008.

Dalby, Ron. *The Alaska Highway: An Insider's Guide*. Bloomington, Ind.: AuthorHouse, 2007.

Dalby, Ron. *Guide to the Alaska Highway*. Birmingham, Ala.: Menasha Ridge Press, 2008.

WEB SITES

The Alaska Highway
http://www.alaska-highway.org/

Alaska Highway Photo Album
http://www.explorenorth.com/library/weekly/aa111398.htm

Alaska Road Traveler Information Service
http://511.alaska.gov/

Driving the Alaska Highway
http://www.outwestnewspaper.com/akhwy.html

The Milepost
http://www.themilepost.com/

PICTURE CREDITS

INDEX

ABOUT THE AUTHOR

PAUL KUPPERBERG is a writer and editor of more than a dozen nonfiction books on topics that include history, popular culture, science, and medicine. He has also written novels, short stories, syndicated newspaper strips, Web animation, humor, and satire, as well as comic, story, and coloring books. He has been an editor of numerous national publications, including a weekly newspaper and a children's magazine. He lives in Connecticut with his wife, Robin, and his son, Max.